SPORTS JOURNALISM

THE INSIDE TRACK

JAMES TONEY

BLOOMSB

Note

While every effort has been made to ensure that the content of this book is
as technically accurate and as sound as possible, neither the authors nor the
publishers can accept responsibility for any injury or loss sustained as a result
of the use of this material.

Published by Bloomsbury Publishing Plc
50 Bedford Square
London WC1B 3DP
www.bloomsbury.com

First edition 2013

ISBN (print): 978-1-4081-7832-4
ISBN (ePDF): 978-1-4081-7833-1
ISBN (EPUB): 978-1-4081-7834-8

A CIP catalogue record for this book is available from the British Library.

Acknowledgements
Cover photographs © Getty
Inside photographs: pp vi (top) and 26 © digitalsport-photoagency/Shutterstock;
p vi (bottom) © Joe Ferrer/Shutterstock; p. 6 © testing/Shutterstock;
pp. 14 and 38 © Natursports/Shutterstock; p. 54 © Neale Cousland/Shutterstock;
p. 68 © Chris Harvey/Shutterstock; p. 88 © skphotography/Shutterstock;
p. 100 © Maxisport/Shutterstock; p. 116 © Shutterstock; and
p. 128 © Photo Works/Shutterstock.
Editor: Nick Ascroft
Commissioned by Kirsty Schaper

This book is produced using paper that is made from wood grown in managed,
sustainable forests. It is natural, renewable and recyclable. The logging and
manufacturing processes conform to the environmental regulations of the
country of origin.

Typeset in 10pt Minion by Saxon Graphics Ltd., Derby

Printed and bound in Great Britain by CPI Group (UK) Ltd, Croydon CR0 4YY
10 9 8 7 6 5 4 3 2 1

CONTENTS

ACKNOWLEDGEMENTS

This project would not have been possible without the help of Sportsbeat colleague Jack Travers, who assisted throughout as we both juggled the demands of an unprecedented year in sports journalism.

Thanks to those colleagues who gave their time and dispensed their knowledge so freely, we didn't just want advice from established names but reporters who have recently started in the industry, whose fresh experiences are more relevant to those seeking to make their first steps into journalism.

Thanks also to my colleague and friend, Sportsbeat's executive editor David Parsons, whose strong opinions on journalism are well known to his staff and, as importantly, good old Mum and Dad, always the first and wisest critics of everything I write.

Sports journalists spend too much time away from home, consumed with their work – so the biggest and final acknowledgement must go to Emma, Ella and Clara for their unstinting support and welcome-home smiles.

1

INTRODUCTION

What is more competitive than the Olympic 100m final? Answer: Covering the Olympic 100m final. Perhaps it is appropriate that a profession that spends so much time judging people against the clock, or each other, should be so difficult to break into. You need to do your training, serve your apprenticeship, persevere, dedicate not deviate and then, when the time comes, seize your chance. A bit of luck along the way helps too – not unlike those you aspire to cover. There's no harm in dreaming big and aiming high, provided you are prepared to start small and lowly.

Every year, sports journalists tell hundreds of thousands of stories: tales of success and failure, triumph and despair, gold medals and 43rd places, no-score bore-draws and five-goal thrillers. They will cover the inspirational and the corrupt. You can bounce from press box to hotel room via dinner in a motorway service station. You can travel to scores of cities and never see the sights. You will know your laptop better than the back of your hand and how to ask for a receipt in 25 different languages.

If you are lucky you might be feted – some journalists have their fan clubs – and you will be hated, because sports journalists certainly have their critics, who, in the digital age, have plenty of options to voice their views that you are biased, incompetent, lazy or, more likely, all three. Don't take this too personally, after all, you will spend plenty of time in your career arguing you are entitled to your opinion and they are too.

Your stomach will frequently be knotted from the anxiety of an approaching deadline, which is why every journalist's toolkit should contain a pack of paracetamol and antacids. You will learn to hate the blank page and your failure to 'nail the intro'. But nothing is better than reading your copy and thinking it can't be bettered. The times it happens can be counted on one hand. Your heart will soar when you get your first byline and sink when you realise that you've made a mistake. Sports journalism is hard yards; it's long hours, it's ruthless and it's utterly addictive.

It can be frustrating and exhilarating in equal measure. Every magical moment you witness is offset by the countless sporting encounters with results that will be quickly forgotten, by even those that participated. Ask a sportswriter to tell you about their most glamorous assignment and you may be entertained with a handful of anecdotes for a few minutes. Ask about the worst assignment and you'll be there for hours. Not that you should feel any twinge of sympathy, after all the saying is that those who ply their trade at the 'back of the book' are meant to be underpaid and over-privileged.

In sports journalism, you will meet your share of amazing people; although to temper your enthusiasm, they will almost always be heavily outweighed by those who are touched with arrogance – some of them may even be other reporters. The hours are unsociable, weekends are nearly always working days and pressure to deliver can be intense. Even on your days off, you can be guaranteed the moment you dig your toes into the sand and take your first sip of ice-cold lager, the phone will beep and a story will break. And if you're a journalist, you should always want to be where the action is – right in the heart of a developing story.

Sports journalism can be relentless. The moment one season concludes, the build-up starts to the one that follows. Within minutes of a team winning the league, or getting relegated, thoughts immediately turn to which player they will sign next or who their next manager might be. The story rarely ends; it can always be continued.

Sport is the heart of the battle for newspaper circulation. It drives internet traffic and fuels ratings wars. Sport is big business, high finance and dirty politics – and when those three combine it should prove a fertile ground for a journalist to do their work. The role of the manager of the England football team is frequently dubbed 'the second most important job in the country', a comment that drives those who cover politics for a living to the point of apoplexy. However, nothing gets the nation talking together like sport, short of a Royal Wedding, Diamond Jubilee or, perhaps a reality-television talent contest. It has the power to generate unrivalled controversy and debate – schedules and pages can be filled with previews and reviews. It is unscripted drama and no industry is better fueled by sensation than the media.

Newspaper sports pages have rapidly expanded in the past decade and now occupy more space, even in newspapers that once were 'sniffy' about those who covered 'muddied oafs and flannelled fools', than world news. It could be argued there is too much space to fill. The internet craves content like a hungry hippo and the result is that sports news becomes overstretched and overexposed. But the demand is there – viewing figures prove sports news is more popular than the general news and switchboards light up fastest at radio stations when the phone-in is discussing the next England manager as opposed to the next prime minister. Sport has become part of human culture to an extent that was previously inconceivable. As former BBC sports editor Mihir Bose once said, 'We have lost religion and found sport.'

While sports journalists are criticised by those who write the serious stuff, it's worth pointing out that the job of political and sports reporters is not that different. Both obsess with who is ahead and who is behind, analyse strategies and tactics, win favour and access, and are targets of spin. Both have to maintain readers' interest and enthusiasm through seasons or campaigns that even at their most exciting will still have the occasional tendency to drag.

The digital age

Sports journalism, however, is fast changing, especially for those who prefer the anonymity of print and the written word as their favoured medium. Opportunities and threats abound in this new digital age. The internet and new technology have created new jobs and new ways of producing sports content. Journalists are no longer leading the national sporting conversation, they are just part of it, with everyone a commentator now on social media.

Some argue journalists are now under such pressure to deliver quick copy and sensational stories that they have lost the art of writing. (Others say that sports journalists are in the pockets of those that control their access – the clubs, agents and public relations industry.) These critics claim that, instead of spellcheckers and the internet raising the standards, they have instead caused them to slide. They fear that computer skills now outweigh journalistic aptitude and that too many stories come from a quick scan of Twitter, rather than from hitting the phones and working their contacts. 'Speed trumps quality,' they moan, and as the saying goes, 'Speed kills'. They believe quotes are king for today's aspiring star reporter. An interview with a footballer, in which they say little of note and only become animated when they are plugging whatever product they are being paid to promote, holds more value than 1000 words of reasoned analysis and colour writing (descriptive pieces, often with opinion threaded in).

Hugh McIlvanney, whose peerless words and faultless turn of phrase make him the much admired sports journalists' sports journalist, summed up these fears when he said:

These days, it can be said of too many in our business that if they went blind, their work wouldn't suffer; but if they went deaf, they couldn't work. They cannot function unless fuelled by quotes.

But there is still a place for good journalism to thrive and opportunities for young talented writers to make their mark.

The internet and 24/7 sports news have changed the way sports reporters work. The old ways are being challenged but you still need to learn the basics and develop your skills. But before you can be a good sports journalist, you need to first learn to be just a good journalist. You need to practise your shorthand, hone your nose for a story and stop thinking like a fan and start thinking like a reporter. You need to embrace the digital age and accept that the traditional media no longer enjoys a monopoly on information. You've also got to be prepared to work hard, stand out from the crowd in a job marketplace where editors can afford to be selective and deliver when you get your chance. In truth, preparing for a career in sports journalism is much like preparing for a career in sport – although, unfortunately, the transfer fees aren't quite so astronomical, the hotels are more budget than five-star and there are no groupies.

Still, it beats working.

2

SAME JOB TITLE, TOTALLY DIFFERENT JOB DESCRIPTION

COVERING THE 1948 AND 2012 LONDON OLYMPICS

London 2012 organisers tried their best to associate their Games with the last Olympics in the British capital in 1948. Both were staged against a backdrop of austerity. In 1948, Britain was recovering from a world war that had left it virtually bankrupt, more than six decades on and the City of London was at the fulcrum of the most serious economic crisis since that time. However, other than gathering beneath the same five-ringed flag, the Games of the XIV Olympiad in 1948 were barely recognisable from the 30th edition of the event (XXX Olympiad) in 2012.

Lord Burghley, who guided the organising committee of the 1948 Games, would struggle to comprehend the enormity of the project masterminded by his successor Lord Coe. Burghley's entire budget was just £760,000, contrasted with Coe's £9.3 billion. Teams travelled to events on public transport, athletes went back to work after their competitions – some even found their pay had been docked – and one of the official sponsors was a popular cigarette brand.

In the 64 years between London's last two Olympics, sports journalism has also changed almost beyond recognition. The job title is the same, but the job description couldn't be more different. In those intervening decades, we have seen television, satellite television and the internet exert their authority over the old media of radio and the written word. Newspapers have also experienced seismic changes. Circulations have fallen, but advances in technology have led to more pages being printed than ever before with later and later deadlines resulting in the inclusion of more and more up-to-date news.

When London staged the Olympics for the second time in 1948, they were the first true media Games – with newspapers, radio, film and television all involved for the first time. More than six decades on and the five-ringed circus rolled up again in the British capital for what was the first digital media Games. The differences between the two events could not have been greater.

In 1948, slightly more than 2000 journalists were accredited and housed in a converted civic hall that boasted a quiet writing room, canteen and bar, which had once been a laundry room. Newspaper proprietor Lord Rothermere donated £7000 to make sure Olympic organisers had appropriate facilities for the world's media. In addition, special permission was obtained to extend the alcohol licence to 11.30 p.m., on the ground that 'normal closure at 10 p.m. would be irksome to foreign correspondents and likely to give an impression of petty and unreasonable restrictions and a bad effect on our campaign to attract foreign tourists.'

In 2012, the facilities were unrivaled with a specially built Main Press Centre and International Broadcast Centre, accommodating 21,000 accredited media workers, operating 24 hours a day, and costing £355 million to build. After the Games, it was envisioned that this facility – dubbed a 'silicon shed' – would be home to new digital businesses to help revive the local economy in Hackney and provide hundreds of new jobs, although that dream has been tempered by the reality of recession. This mini village included a catering outlet that served 50,000 meals a day and its own high street, complete with bank, newsagent, travel agent, gym and two bars. Journalists could also order takeaway food, delivered to their desks.

Many media workers from the host nation were disappointed not to receive any accreditation, with the British Olympic Association (BOA) reporting there were 4000 applications for the 500 passes they had available for written-media workers from the United Kingdom. In addition, it's estimated up to 10,000 unaccredited media workers, many representing broadcasters without rights to the Games, were also in the city. These journalists came from almost every competing nation, forming the largest gathering of media workers ever assembled in one place.

In 1948, results were distributed to the press by Boy Scouts; in 2012, a specially designed intranet delivered timings and placings within seconds of an event concluding, although paper copies were still delivered, this time by volunteers dressed head to toe by the official clothing sponsor rather than Scouts with their sewed-on badges and toggles.

Any journalist will tell you the most important thing when attending an event, maybe after recceing the food and drink options, is working out how you can file your copy. The best-written story in the world or an agenda-setting news story means little if you can't get it back from your assignment to your office on time or ahead of your rivals.

In 1948, a complete telephone exchange was installed adjacent to the press office and four telephones were assigned for overseas calls – which had to be booked a day in advance. Many reporters filed by telegram. After composing their message, they would drop it down a gutter pipe that ran from the window of the press bar to a station manned by volunteers on bicycles. The couriers would then ride to a teleprinter operator, who keyed the story into a machine from which it was translated into Morse code and transmitted to the relevant country.

More than 60 years on and today's journalists have no excuses for missing their deadline. Every press tribune seat (in the areas reserved for journalists) was cabled to give reporters access to a high-speed internet connection and the results intranet system on their laptop, although organisers were criticised for the £150 charge they applied. Wi-Fi was available in media lounges, where refreshments were laid on, and many also used wireless dongles. Larger agencies set up their own office space in the Main Press Centre – with Reuters and Agence France-Presse both sending more than 100 staff, from reporters and photographers to editors and technicians. They installed their own networks, allowing them to work as effectively in the heart of the Olympic Park as they could if they were sitting at their own desks.

Journalists who covered the 1948 Olympics recall their press centre being filled with a cacophony of sound, the clack and pings of typewriters, crescendoing as deadlines approached. In 2012 the main writing room, with more than 800 desks, hummed quietly as journalists tapped on the keyboards of their laptops.

The only way to see the action in 1948 was to get out to the venues; in 2012, a live feed from all sports was beamed into the Main Press Centre. A journalist sitting in East London could watch a press conference in Weymouth and cover the sailing even though they were 150 miles away.

Sir Arthur Conan Doyle and the 1908 Olympics

It would certainly be interesting to know what Sir Arthur Conan Doyle, the author of Sherlock Holmes novels, would make of such facilities. He was part of the Olympic press pack in 1908, when London first staged the Games, commissioned to cover a storied marathon, won by American Johnny Hayes but famous for the performance of Italian baker Dorando Pietri, who led the race into the stadium but collapsed and was helped across the line, leading to his disqualification. 'I do not often do journalistic work,' Conan Doyle wrote in his memoirs, 'but on the occasion of the Olympic Games of 1908 I was tempted, chiefly by the offer of an excellent seat, to do the marathon report for the *Daily Mail*.'

Photography at the Olympics

Power, beauty and athletic prowess. The Olympic Games have long generated some of the most enduring and iconic images of sport from Bob Beamon sailing into the air to record a world long jump record in Mexico City to a wide-eyed Usain Bolt crossing the line in Beijing to claim the 100m title. The photographic rights for the 1948 Games were sold to a consortium of leading picture agencies, which came together to form the Olympic Photo Association. In return for exclusive copyright of images, the association had to make their photos available for sale to all newspapers and prints had to go on sale to the public as soon as they had been published. They employed just 40 photographers – who had special armbands giving them access to the field of play – to cover all events at the Games. An exhibition of Games photography was set up in the Palace of Engineering near Wembley Stadium. It became a popular tourist attraction with foreign visitors buying more than 5000 prints.

In London, hundreds of photographers from around the world attended the 2012 Games. They had access to camera loan, repair and various other support services. Inside competition areas were dedicated photo positions with workspaces to facilitate quick access to filing facilities. Lighting levels inside arenas were agreed in advance and photographers were assisted by 55 paid photo operations staff and a further 600 dedicated volunteers. In advance of the Games, photographers scouted the best positions, with three world press briefings held for accredited media people. Organisers secured dedicated positions to capture marathon runners as they crossed Westminster Bridge beside the House of Commons, cyclists as they entered The Mall by Buckingham Palace, horse riders competing in Greenwich Park, framed by the skyscrapers of Docklands, and beach volleyball players attempting a spike against the backdrop of Whitehall.

Unlike some sporting events – which try to claim and restrict distribution of images – the International Olympic Committee (IOC) allow accredited photographers to publish and distribute their images on any platform, without time delay for editorial purposes, and made no copyright claim on the pictures. Leading sports photo agency Getty Images were not even founded when the 1948 Games were staged but are now established as the official photographic agency of the IOC and at the forefront of sports photography. They had more than 100 staff covering the 2012 Olympics, with photographers and photo editors at every venue, from where they promised to distribute pictures quicker than ever before. The moment an image was captured it was sent wirelessly to the laptop of a dedicated photo editor, who adjusted it, captioned it and uploaded the image on to Getty's password-accessed website. Subscriber media could then download the picture into their own system and have it ready for publication, in print or online, less than five minutes after the image was taken.

Getty also pioneered the use of 3D and 360-degree camera techniques to record footage and, along with other agencies, installed remote cameras at every venue, so they could capture dramatic moments from right inside the goalmouth at Wembley Stadium and underwater at the Olympic pool. The agency also used robotic cameras to capture the Games from unique perspectives, creating photos that were no longer just something pretty to look at. Using cameras that created 360-degree images, online content was created that readers could engage with and manipulate: rotating through the complete sphere of the image or zooming in to the point that they could identify one individual in a crowd. In the stadium, a helicam hovered in the skies taking bird's-eye-view shots from above and time-lapse cameras were installed.

In 1948, the majority of people learned about what had happened at the Games in their morning or evening newspapers or on radio – with 11 million British households owning wireless sets but just 90,000 having access to a television. Now that television dominates, broadcasters around the world paid nearly £1 billion for rights to the 2012 Games, while in a bid to increase their global reach, the IOC allowed YouTube to stream live action to almost all countries across Asia and Africa. The BBC was asked to pay £1000 for the rights to transmit the Games on radio and television in 1948, by London 2012 this fee had increased to £64 million.

In 1948, Olympic organisers had even discussed whether the Games would benefit from the presence of television cameras, although one of the senior organisers, Sir Arthur Elvin, was determined the BBC should broadcast the event. In total, 70 hours of Olympic action was broadcast, including seven hours in one single day. In 2012, the BBC broadcast all 5000 hours of competition through their various channels, including live streaming on their website. The coverage was designed to ensure audiences never missed a moment, with on-demand and catch-up services available so those interested could stay up to date wherever they were, whenever they wanted to. Their flagship channel, BBC One, cleared its entire schedule from breakfast until the early hours of the morning and dedicated every minute to the Games.

While London 2012 saw broadcasts in high definition and 3D, the 1948 Games were the subject of the first feature-length documentary shot in colour. Producer J. Arthur Rank paid £20,000 for exclusive film rights and to protect his rights, ticket holders and the press were banned from taking moving pictures of any kind – a restriction that continues but now to protect the multimillion-pound investment of international broadcasters.

The Olympics in the digital age

The differences between the scale of the 1948 and 2012 Olympics and the media that covered them underline some of the challenges facing journalists today. Since even the 2008 Games in Beijing, the digital landscape has totally changed, with the arrival of the tablet, rapid penetration of smartphones and growing use of internet-connected televisions. Sports journalism is a constantly evolving industry, by the time London next stages the Olympics it will be virtually unrecognisable again. If you read the above description of press operations after the 2016 Rio Olympics or before the 2020 Games, you'll see how much it has dated.

Looking ahead to the 2012 London Olympics, Reuters editor-in-chief David Schlesinger noted in a speech to the IOC's press commission in 2009:

> Chances are, a lot of compelling video will be shot on mobile phones and uploaded on sharing sites on the internet within minutes. Chances are, the first report of a result out of a stadium won't be Reuters, AP [Associated Press] or AFP [Agence France-Presse]. Chances are the first report of a result will be one of 1572 (to pick a number at random) Twitterers sitting in the stadium banging the result out in a tweet from their mobile phone. And since tweets can aggregated and can be searched by keyword – who is the journalist? What is the media organisation? Who has control?

He added:

> Fundamentally, the old media won't control news dissemination in the future. And organisations can't control access using old forms of accreditation any more. The four years between Summer Olympics can see several generations of change in new media.

But even in this multimedia age, it would be foolish to say there is no longer a place for the written word, which can add depth, context and analysis. But sports journalists now must try to tell the story behind the story, rather than just the story. In a media landscape where information is created in huge and impenetrable quantities, the sports journalist, with his or her expert knowledge and contacts, is still needed to decide what is and isn't newsworthy. They will continue to ask difficult questions, hold people to account and seek to reveal stories others want to suppress.

In an age when news travels quicker than Usain Bolt, a sports journalist has to be cuter than an American figure skater, be more nimble than a Russian gymnast and, when covering events like the Olympics, have the stamina levels of a 50km race walker.

Fig 2.1   Main Press Centre, home to over 5,000 written-press journalists during the London 2012 Olympics

3

THE EVER-CHANGING SHAPE OF SPORTS MEDIA

There are press passes to sort, travel to book, people to schmooze and placate, expenses to query and sign-off and budgets to balance while somewhere in the middle of all this semi-organised chaos there are pages to plan, events to cover and stories to break. Sports desks take on different shapes and sizes depending on the publication. On a smaller, usually weekly title, the role of sports editor covers everything from attending events, writing reports, drawing pages and liaising with contributors.

However, a sports editor on a larger title – or the editor on a specialist sporting publication – could be assisted by a number of senior editorial executives, collectively known as the backbench. Job titles could include deputy sports editor, the number two and in charge in the editor's absence, sports news editor and assistant sports news editor, responsible for day to day management of the desk and planning, and a chief subeditor, the key figure in the production operation who is responsible for a subs desk. The backbench manages all content from text to images, which are in turn managed by the picture desk.

Some subeditors have staff contracts but others work as freelancers or casuals and come in for shifts around peak production times. Larger titles will also employ a night sports editor who takes responsibility for the desk in the evening through to the time the final edition goes to press in the early hours of the morning, although the editor is likely to remain around for major events and will always be in contact should a major story develop. Editorial staff will be further swelled by senior reporters, including a chief sportswriter who usually contributes a regular column, and lead correspondents – often referred to as 'number ones' – such as the football correspondent, cricket correspondent, rugby union correspondent or racing correspondent. They, in turn, may be supported by deputies.

Most people only specialise in a sport once they've spent time on general assignment. Increasingly, some specialists have a background in their sport, for example former England cricket captain Michael Atherton who has moved effortlessly into the media. It's also not unknown for reporters to swap specialisms – Alan Lee switched from his high-profile role as cricket correspondent at *The Times* to become their racing correspondent. Some reporters might combine primary responsibility for one sport, such as tennis or athletics, but provide general coverage when that event is not in season. Others will have a more roving brief, contributing features or big-name interviews. Reporters will also be divided by region, with certain teams and clubs on their patch – so that they can work harder and more effectively to develop stories and contacts.

On weekly or regional newspapers, most reporters probably base themselves in the office. On national titles, most will work remotely and only visit the office occasionally. However, most larger titles always have 'duty reporters', who work on the desk, following up stories that break and supporting correspondents in the field from the office. Additional staff, again frequently office-based, might be dedicated to providing online coverage, rewriting stories that come in from wire agencies such as the Press Association, Reuters and Agence France-Presse, monitoring other media, live blogging and getting an initial story running that will be followed by a more considered version in print. Some newspapers use different teams for their online and print output. Others, increasing in number, are more integrated and staff will work both online and in print.

Freelance journalists

Papers will also use freelance journalists or stringers to provide coverage from less mainstream sports, such as sailing or rowing. Some of these may be paid an annual retainer; others will provide copy on a more ad hoc basis, around major events or press conferences. They may also find that interviews with big stars from their sport are assigned to their paper's non-specialist feature writers. Freelancers often work for multiple outlets and operate as one-man or woman agencies, with responsibility for their own travel arrangements and press accreditation. To make this pay, they require several commissions – or orders – and must juggle the challenge of keeping their different paymasters happy, which sounds easy until three different papers ask for exactly the same thing at exactly the same time and each expects to take priority. Freelancers will also be used extensively to produce match coverage, although this is increasingly outsourced to agencies such as the Press Association or Sportsbeat, which also offer page-production services in which their production staff lay out pages to the design specification of a client title and then send them completed and ready for publication. In recent years, freelancers have been especially squeezed by these agencies, which have economies of scale that give them more margin to strike content deals with budget-conscious editors.

Many sports departments have desk managers or secretaries to assist with organisational tasks, from sorting out press passes, or accreditation, to sourcing travel plans for reporters. They will also be responsible for briefing freelance reporters and giving them their orders ahead of assignments, which for ease is almost exclusively done by email. Only those reporters covering big matches or feature games will get called by a senior journalist to discuss potential lines and angles.

David Jordan, who completed his National Council for the Training of Journalists (NCTJ) qualification and joined the *Grimsby Telegraph* before moving to Sportsbeat, where he is responsible for their match-day live service, says:

> Getting the logistics and planning right is one of the biggest parts of the job. On a busy Saturday afternoon, we have well over 150 football match reports coming into the office, nearly the same again with rugby union and possibly ten cricket reports. They all arrive at virtually the same time and if that process isn't planned in detail we'd never fulfill our contractual responsibilities.

The sports editor is responsible for the entire department and will attend a daily news conference of senior executives across all sections that is chaired by the editor. It is here the agenda for the publication is decided and pages assigned. Sports editors will also spend time developing contacts, negotiating interviews or attempting to sign-up guest columnists. Forward planning is vital. Coverage of big events such as the FIFA World Cup or the Olympics is planned months in advance and the expense of covering such events means sport has one of the biggest budgets – set by the managing editor – of any section in a newspaper.

Smaller titles, such as regional dailies or weekly newspapers, operate on the same basis but with fewer staff and those responsible for management of the section may also have reporting commitments. They will focus on events in their circulation area and will largely be reliant on agencies to provide coverage of national and international events, if they believe them relevant to their readers. Regional and weekly titles also publish a large amount of contributed material, provided, usually free of charge, by club and sport press officers, which could include results, reports and news stories. Increasingly those in the regional press work across several local titles, perhaps with responsibility for a daily and a number of weekly free and paid-for papers, whose deadlines are staggered across the week.

In recent years, as a cost-saving measure, many daily national newspapers have merged their sports desk with that of their Sunday sister publication, which previously had a stand-alone staff. At the 2000 Olympics in Sydney, the *Independent* and the *Independent on Sunday* both had an athletics correspondent each. At London 2012, however, one person worked the role for both newspapers, with his coverage also running in the *Independent*'s daily sister title *i* and the *London Evening Standard*, which is now part of the same group.

Some British Sunday newspapers still retain their own reporting and senior editorial team – for example, the *Mail on Sunday* and the *Sunday Times* – and those that have stopped short of full integration often share production resources with their daily stablemate.

However, seven-day operations – with the associated cost savings they bring – are now common. Britain's two biggest tabloid newspapers, the *Sun* and *Daily Mirror*, are both now run by the same management and editorial team on every day of the week.

The sports desk will be responsible for all sports content in a newspaper, although its reporters may contribute crossover pieces that appear in other sections when relevant, for example a sports-related business story for the financial pages. Sport is traditionally published at the 'back of the book' but some titles now run stand-alone sports sections. *The Times* has a popular football supplement, published on Mondays during the season, while one-off specials are also produced around major events. Traditionally, Sunday was the strongest day for newspaper sales and, considering the bulk of sporting action takes place on a Saturday, the papers put additional emphasis on sport. However, in recent years Saturdays have become the biggest newspaper-buying day. In April 2012, the 10 UK national dailies together sold an average of 10,077,007 copies on Saturdays while the combined sale of the 10 national Sundays was 8,045,429. Saturday papers are now packed with previews and interviews that look ahead to the sporting weekend. In addition, betting companies are now one of the biggest commercial supporters of sports sections and more and more content is being devised to leverage this relationship, with tipping columns – not just covering racing – common in every paper.

Sports-only newspapers

There is a strong tradition for sports-only newspapers on the continent, such as *L'Équipe* in France, *MARCA* in Spain and *La Gazzetta dello Sport* in Italy. However, because of the strength of sports coverage in the national and regional UK press, sports-only titles have struggled to gain a foothold in a crowded media marketplace – the UK has 10 national dailies.

Sports-only newspaper *Sport First* launched in 1998 but folded six years later, although it is credited with forcing many national titles to take sport more seriously. Whereas the *Sportsman*, an ill-conceived seven-days-a-week sports paper, launched in 2006, folded just seven months later. The UK's only daily sports paper is now the *Racing Post*, although its coverage is dedicated to horse racing and sports betting. There were talks to launch *Sporting Life*, a former racing paper with strong name recognition, as a daily sports title but the idea was scrapped while sample editions were still being produced.

Sport is a weekly free magazine, now owned by sports radio station TalkSport, that has won industry praise and there are two weekly newspapers dedicated to the coverage of football – the *Non-League Paper*, for matches below the Football League, and the *Football Paper*, which is targeted at supporters of Football League clubs. The same publisher also produces the *Rugby Paper*, again published on Sundays, and the *Cricket Paper*, which reviews and previews the English cricket scene and hits the news stands on Wednesdays. There also remains a market for monthly magazines covering sport, with the strongest sellers in the specialist areas of running/fitness, cycling, football, cricket and triathlon. These magazines don't just report the action but review products and publish tips for amateurs who participate in the sports.

Online sports desks don't tend to be as rigid in their structure. Their editors, reporters and content producers take responsibility for site maintenance, load stories via a content management system, link their articles to related stories and external sites, write headlines and live blogs, create picture galleries and manage comments, user-generated content and Twitter feeds.

Most websites, even those attached to well-known brands of sports media, have a small staff and a heavy reliance on agency copy, which often leads to accusations that many sites look exactly the same because their content is almost identical. In contrast, BBC Sport's online staff contribute a range of multimedia content to a range of platforms. They might attend an event and write a quick report for the website while also providing broadcast content – audio and video – that might be used in any of the organisation's numerous outlets from regional radio to network programming. The growing trend and focus on multimedia skills (*see* Chapter 10), means editors need journalists that can turnaround quick and accurate copy and are as comfortable working with moving pictures as they are with words.

Numerous sports websites also rely heavily on contributed content, although much of it is provided free of charge by trainee journalists looking to get a platform for their work. Goal.com is one of the world's most visited football websites with a huge number of contributors producing hundreds of stories a day. Aspiring writers on the site go through a series of online training procedures – explaining style and story sourcing – and upload their stories on to a content management system. They are then checked by paid subeditors, who work remotely in six-hour shifts, before being published. Some of the material is originally sourced but much is aggregated from other content providers and credited accordingly. This aggregation of content leads to accusations of cut-and-paste journalism.

Bleacher Report is another of the web's most visited sports destinations – although its model for content collection has attracted criticism. It relies on being supplied with free copy, describing a typical writer as 'a guy who works by day and is a 49ers fan by night'. Some are put off by articles that are heavy on opinion and light on facts, but with 20 million monthly unique visitors, the site is certainly alluring to advertisers. In recent months, they have added some professional journalists to their roster of writers and the site still ranks ahead of big-brand names in sports media such as Entertainment and Sports Programming Network (ESPN) and Yahoo. For the aspiring journalist looking to develop a portfolio and get some writing experience, these sorts of site can give you vital experience. However, always try to seek feedback from experienced journalists whenever possible and constantly compare your work to more established names in the industry. Self-publishing opens up a world of opportunities, but it can always allow sloppy habits to develop.

Increasingly clubs, sports, governing bodies or major tournaments want to control their message and have become publishers themselves, with websites, official magazines or television stations as part of their output. While they are put together in much the same way as independent media, with editors, journalists, story lists and a production process, they stay away from publishing anything critical of the organisation funding their budget and work closely with the media department to ensure content is presented in an appropriate way. Leading associations such as UEFA, FIFA or the International Rugby Board also have official websites and publications, from match programmes to magazines. They often buy in content from agencies but will supplement it with their own material, especially during major events.

During the Olympic Games, the organisers ran a news service, which was made available to accredited media to use free of charge to supplement their own reporting. It operated likes a news agency with a central editorial team, run by experienced journalists, and liaised with venue-reporting teams that were headed by an editor but included sports specialists and volunteer journalists who provided news reports, previews, reviews and flash quotes in a variety of languages.

Press agencies

Agencies have always played an important role in newsgathering. Key organisations include international wire services like Reuters, Agence France-Presse and Associated Press, national agencies like the Press Association in the UK, Agenzia Nazionale Stampa Associata (ANSA) in Italy and Canadian Press, sports press agencies like Sportsbeat in the UK and Sport-Informations-Dienst (SID) in Germany and sports picture agencies like Getty Images or Action Images. Some agencies provide a wire service, publishing all their content to client media companies. Others provide bespoke editorial feeds for clients, for example in just one sport or to a certain geographic region.

All agencies have diversified in recent years, moving away from a total focus on newspapers to provide a range of editorial services to new media such as websites and mobile phone companies. The growth in sports data, results, statistics, tables etc., fueled in turn by the growth of sports betting and games such as fantasy football, has put a value on the distribution of sports data by media companies. Most agencies have also developed specific products for new media, from syndicated live blogs to multimedia packages, both audio and video, so that more and more journalists with broadcast skills are now working for companies traditionally associated with print media.

Most major events have strict controls over who can access press facilities and demand for passes normally exceeds supply. Some events and competitions are licensed, for which news outlets have to hold a central pass, issued for example by the Premier League, to be able to apply for individual match accreditation. Allocation for international competitions such as the Olympic Games or FIFA World Cup is decided by national governing bodies, such as the British Olympic Association (BOA) or the Football Association. BOA received more than 4000 applications for the 500 written-press passes available for the London 2012 Games. They employed a panel of respected journalists to advise them in this process and media was prioritised based on their circulation and previous commitment to the coverage of Olympic sport. Written-press accreditation carries no charge – although journalists can be charged, depending on the event, for use of facilities such as Wi-Fi. Entry for broadcasters depends on whether they are rights-holders and access will be denied or limited to those that have not paid to screen the event.

Sports event organisers continue to struggle to define where sports websites come into this equation – considering their content is a mix of text and multimedia. Increasingly, journalists writing for websites are being accepted into the press box – because their sites' visitors can often exceed circulations of newspapers. But some organisers refuse to allow those with new-media credentials, viewing them as competitors of their own official website, a view that has become blurred considering the number of newspapers that now place equal significance on their journalists providing online copy.

There have been several disputes between sporting events and journalists over the terms now applied to media accreditation that some view as limiting the freedom of the press. Many newspapers and agencies boycotted the opening day of the 2011–2012 Football League season because of small print on their press credentials that prevented them providing rolling match coverage. Several agencies, including Reuters and Associated Press, suspended coverage of the Australian cricket team in a dispute over terms of accreditation to cover matches. Cricket Australia, the governing body for cricket in Australia, had imposed limits on what could be published on websites not owned by an established newspaper or sports magazine, essentially preventing independent websites from any access to coverage – either their own or bought in – from inside the ground. This forced the sites to cover matches by watching them on television, while the news agencies accused the accreditation terms of not respecting editorial critique of the sport.

In many cases, a compromise is finally established but newspapers have been known to omit names of sponsors from copy and purposefully not publish photos that give prominence to shirt sponsors in retaliation. It is also not uncommon for sports journalists to be banned from accreditation if they have written something that upsets a club or sport. The journalist involved often wears this as a badge of honour and will always find a way of continuing his or her coverage without official sanction.

Accreditation

Press credentials usually give access to a ground, media lounge and an area where journalists can interview players or athletes post-match or competition. At Wimbledon tennis tournament, some press accreditation gives access to the Centre Court press box and some only allows access to the grounds and media centre, where journalists can watch games on television and attend press conferences. Attend the British Open Golf and your pass might restrict you to the course and media centre or you may get a preferential credential that allows you to walk inside the ropes. At the Olympics, some journalists have a pass that admits them to all events, whereas others are restricted to certain sports or venues.

Press accreditation is rarely given to freelancers not known to organisers without a letter of commission from the editor of a respected media outlet. Applications for press credentials open well in advance of an event. For the Olympic Games, the accreditation process starts nearly two years before the actual event. Whereas, press officers at football clubs usually require 48 hours' notice of attendance, with many leagues now having an online system, accessed by password, where journalists can apply for passes.

Press boxes can be daunting places to walk into for the first time. Everyone seems to know each other and you get the feeling they are eyeing the new girl or boy on the scene with distrust. It's good to be friendly, introduce yourself and mention the company you are working for and be aware it can be a stressful environment, especially when deadlines are pressing.

Frank Smith, who graduated from his NCTJ course three years ago and is now a sports reporter for the *Watford Observer*, remembers:

> I was only a year or so out of school when I first went into a press box at a Football League ground. I thought I didn't belong there and was very nervous. I soon realised that other journalists aren't that scary and the competitive camaraderie is now something I really enjoy about the job.

In the last decade, the biggest growth area of sports media has been public relations, or PR – and increasingly those PR agencies and communications departments at clubs, leagues and associations are seeking out journalism skills when they recruit because they see themselves as content providers. Only a few journalists can claim they don't require good contacts with PR people to do their job – it's a symbiotic relationship and a trainee reporter under the misapprehension of holding the power will soon be in for a shock. The truth is journalists and PR people need each other in equal measure. PR companies control a great deal of interest to a journalist – most predominantly access – which is all important in an age when aspiring footballers who aren't yet teenagers have agents,.

As mentioned, PR companies see themselves as content providers – they will provide editorial material, sprinkled with a key message about a sponsorship or endorsement, direct to the media. The tolerance for this sort of branded coverage has only increased. Global sports sponsorship is worth £5 billion a year and rising – an increase of nearly 50 per cent in the decade up to the London 2012 Olympics. Indeed, sport accounts for 80 per cent of global sponsorship. That's because sport is a global language, understood regardless of background and able to penetrate borders and age groups. Association with a sporting event, team or athlete can transform the fortunes of a brand and sponsorship can provide longevity of recognition. Sport is news 24/7 – and it's often front-page news as well. It never stops and brands have really woken up to that. The growth in sports PR over the past five years has been phenomenal. Rather than waiting for the next World Cup, Olympics or Ashes series, brands will increasingly begin to create their own events, giving more power to the PR agencies that control them.

Brands that associate themselves with sports stars have also seen the effects of what happens should those who receive their endorsement fall from grace, such as Tiger Woods. He is the world's first billionaire sportsman, his success breaking down stereotypes of golf as a sport for older, white, upper-class men and making him an icon for young people and minorities. Woods rewrote the sports-marketing rule book and his global appeal proved that the right sports stars can be used to market any product – from watches, banks and razors to video games, credit cards and sports equipment. But many of these sponsors were quick to desert him when unsavoury headlines arose about his private life because they claimed he was no longer the right representative for their brand.

Sports journalists in the written press have more profile than they did 50 years ago. Their opinion is regularly sought by television and radio, while sports sections in newspapers have exploded in size – when England won the World Cup in 1966, the story was covered in just six pages by the majority of national titles but imagine what would happen now. Half a century ago, it was also likely the journalists earned more than those they reported on – but now the balance has greatly shifted.

Sports coverage in newspapers

Football dominates sports coverage, according to a study of the sports pages of 80 newspapers from 22 countries by researchers at two German universities and the respected sports website Play the Game. Their findings claimed that nearly 78 per cent of all articles about sport focused on athletes, coaches, teams and their performances. In contrast, only 2.7 per cent of the coverage examined sports politics, while sports finance and economics were the topics of 3.1 per cent of the nearly 20,000 articles studied. Football accounted for 40 per cent of global sports coverage but that percentage rose to between 50 and 85 per cent in Europe and South America. Men's sport also dominated. Of the articles written about individual players or athletes, more than 80 per cent were about men. Indeed, the research indicated newspapers don't just focus on male sports but also that their articles are written overwhelmingly by male journalists – 92 per cent of the stories studied carried the byline of a male sportswriter.

Sport can also be parochial – newspapers tend to focus, understandably, on stories within their own patch, be that local, regional or national. However, the coverage of international sport by national newspapers is increasing. The survey also indicated a widespread tendency for sports journalists to use very few sources in their articles. Indeed, in more than 40 per cent of all the articles, only one source was quoted – a stark contrast to a similar survey carried out for general news stories. Even more interesting, and perhaps concerning, is one in four articles is presented to readers without indicating any sources at all. Coaches and athletes make up about half of the sources, followed by representatives of clubs and sports officials and only rarely do journalists use experts from outside sport.

4

PRIOR PLANNING PREVENTING POOR PERFORMANCE

Newsrooms don't tend to run like military operations. Order and efficiency are replaced by piles of newspapers, empty coffee cups (once upon a time – full ashtrays) and an atmosphere of controlled chaos. Many journalists would argue it is precisely this environment that enables them to do their best work. The fear and panic of an onrushing deadline are perfect stimulants for creative juices to flow. So the appliance of *'Proper Planning and Preparation Prevents Poor Performance'*, the old British Army 'Six Ps' adage – since adopted by management consultants everywhere – might seem a strange one. However, when it comes to sports journalism, to shamelessly steal again from one of those management self-help books, failing to prepare often means preparing to fail.

The first lesson at any journalism school is usually related to the 'Five Ws':

- *Who* is it about?
- *What* happened?
- *Where* did it take place?
- *When* did it take place?
- *Why* did it happen?

The advent of Twitter, a 24-hour news culture and the rapid reactions of online media have diminished the importance of the above. Telling the story behind the story is often the challenge now for the print journalist, when story cycles can be measured in minutes rather than hours and days.

Being first with the news of sports results is all but impossible – sports news is a different matter. Someone with a smartphone, laptop or tablet and a Twitter account will always beat a story that's been filed, edited and then published. However, it's worth remembering that a recent study showed that only 9 per cent of Twitter users get their news from the microblogging site. This compares with 36 per cent who use news websites, 32 per cent who use search engines, and 29 per cent who use news-aggregation sites.

Indeed, researchers from the Pew Research Centre in the United States claimed that when news is shared via Twitter or Facebook, it is usually stories more unusual or viral. Martin Kaymer's trick-shot ace at the 2012 Par 3 Tournament was viewed by more than a million people on YouTube within 48 hours of occurring and most of the traffic was referred from social media. It might be that many people first learned of big stories, such as the tragic death of British IndyCar driver Dan Wheldon, on social media but they quickly navigated to more trusted news sources for depth and colour, proving that quality, trusted and accurate reporting is still essential.

While the 'Five Ws' might no longer be quite as significant, sports journalism still has the 'Two Rs' – *Reading and Research* – and they are key to success. Journalists need to be huge consumers of content across a range of media, from traditional print to online. Specialist correspondents have the luxury of drilling down their knowledge to know a lot about a little, unlike those reporters who find themselves bouncing across a number of sports.

Arguing your case

The impartiality that applies to news stories doesn't always transfer to stories at the 'back of the book', where the majority of sports sections are published. Even when providing a balanced report, a journalist might have to describe a particular athlete's 'nightmare run of form' or a player's 'disappointing' performance. However, when expressing an opinion as a journalist, it is important to back it up with fact. Your copy will also be read by the people you are writing about so expect them to question you on it if they don't agree with what you've said and be prepared to argue your case about why you wrote what you did. You can say, 'United's strikers are letting the side down' but if cross-examined you will need to back that up with, 'Well they've scored 4 goals in 12 games and 2 of those were penalties'.

Fans will also be quick to question your objectivity – it's true that every Liverpool fan thinks their local paper is biased towards Everton and vice versa. But sports journalists know they are writing for an informed audience and fans of clubs, teams or individuals will gleefully point out a mistake or inaccuracy. This is the case even more so now than ever before with comments sections on websites making it much easier and quicker to vent your spleen as opposed to sitting down, writing a letter, putting a stamp on it and taking it to the postbox.

This background research is even more relevant when covering less mainstream sports, especially around events such as the Olympics. Followers of curling are probably a pretty passionate bunch used to, and likely to be a little annoyed by, receiving little coverage of their sport, apart from every four years. And the majority of sportswriters who cover curling at an Olympics probably don't see a match from one Games to the next. That makes reading and research all the more important. Understanding the basic rules, scoring, key personalities, dominant teams and the history of the sport is vital. It would be impossible to have the depth of knowledge of a specialist correspondent or those who follow the sport regularly but making an effort to know it's a 'house' not a 'target' and a 'skip' not a 'captain', is both expected and appreciated. Also, when someone yells 'die' they are not being needlessly aggressive, just asking for their colleagues to stop sweeping their rock.

Any journalist should consume a large diet of news on a daily basis – and that doesn't just mean the back pages. Sport cannot divorce itself from the world in which it operates, as proven by the exclusion of South African teams and athletes from world sport because of the reviled regime of apartheid in their country between 1948 and 1994 or the cancellation of the 2011 Bahrain Grand Prix because of civil unrest in the Arab kingdom. A big breaking news story often has a sporting angle. After the September 11 terrorist attacks, following five days of conjecture, the 2001 Ryder Cup was finally called off and rescheduled for the following year and when terrorists coordinated shooting and bombing attacks across Mumbai in 2008, sports journalists immediately questioned whether the 2010 Commonwealth Games in Delhi were under threat.

The problems of a company or individual reported in the financial papers could also have a sporting hook. Do they sponsor a team or a league? When financier Allen Stanford was arrested for fraud in 2012, he was a major supporter and sponsor of a number of sports, principally cricket, tennis and golf. When a cloud of volcanic ash caused air traffic to be suspended across swathes of Europe in 2011, a smart sports journalist should have beem thinking, 'Which events might be affected and will any athletes be stranded?'

Sports journalists have been first on the scene to cover some of the biggest news of recent years from the hostage crisis that dominated the Munich Olympics in 1972 to the pipe bomb that exploded 24 years later during the Atlanta Games. Those football journalists who turned up to Valley Parade in Bradford on 11 May, 1985, Heysel a few weeks later or Hillsborough on 15 April, 1989, did so thinking of their 'on the whistle' reports, quotes reaction pieces and player ratings. However, they were soon covering events that would dominate the front pages and be at the top of the news bulletins for days to come.

It is impossible as a sports journalist to think your world only revolves around sport – decisions made by the European Court of Justice can have lasting impact on your reporting work, the Bosman ruling being a case in point, a technical point of law now known by every football correspondent.

Hugh McIlvanney said in an address to students at Leicester's De Montfort University:

> The aspiring journalist should identify people who are good at the trade and learn from them. And always, always do a lot of reading.
>
> In sports journalism specifically, I think it is imperative to be very conscious of the need to keep in touch with the wider concerns of the world, with real life, if you like. Do not fall for the insularity that sometimes afflicts sports journalism.

It certainly pays not to disagree with McIlvanney, arguably the finest British sportswriter of all time and the only one so far to have been voted Britain's Journalist of the Year. Simply, the more you read, the more you learn. This is as quoted by Steven Downes, secretary of the Sports Journalists' Association on their official website, which is required reading for any aspiring sports reporter:

> Read Bill Bryson's *Letters from a Small Island*, which is a good start and also his English language primer. Read *Eats, Shoots and Leaves* by Lynne Truss, especially if you are one of the near-illiterates who has yet to work out where capital letters ought to go in a sentence or that plurals don't require apostrophes.
>
> Read *Scoop* by Evelyn Waugh. Read *All the President's Men* by Woodward and Bernstein. Read *Tell Me No Lies* by John Pilger. Read *Pratt of the Argus* by David Nobbs.
>
> Read Dickens. Read Wodehouse. Read Kingsley Amis. Read Graham Greene.

The more content you consume, the more you might spot angles that could have been overlooked. You will pick up, by a process of osmosis, different writing styles, different ways of weaving in quotes or information or statistics. Also, when looking for a 'line' – the best angle to lead a story on – it is vital to have knowledge of recent comments made by the person you are interviewing. But you don't always get time to prepare for interviews. An unexpected opportunity could open up and you need to know enough to be able to wing it and still come out with usable material.

Monitor your rivals closely and don't just read but listen and watch. Radio and television journalists often get some of the best stories because, as rights-holders, they sometimes get better access. No editor wants to run similar or rehash stories that have already appeared in rival publications, so targeting questions to elicit fresh answers and new information is key. If you've missed the best story first time around, you can always try to get the best follow-up, move the story on or, sometimes even more satisfyingly, shoot it down.

It is only 10 years since football reporters would turn up at matches, groaning under the weight of lever-arch files, clippings folders and reference books that could give them the information they needed about previous performances, clubs, date of births and international honours. The internet has lessened their load considerably, although a scan of recent Wikipedia entries for the England cricket team revealed a startling number of factual inaccuracies, underlining the importance of using trusted sources – in particular official sites – as key reference points.

Official websites often carry a sanitised version of the news but their statistical sections can normally be relied upon. Although, trust your own judgement if you witnessed player A scoring last week and it's not listed. Go with that – in the millions of words written and figures published about sport there are always mistakes. However, it is worth remembering that you can't always get online at venues – so don't rely on finding out this information when you get there. Do your research in advance. Journalists now spend their time moaning about Wi-Fi strength. If you are filing a report as soon as an event finishes, known as an 'on the whistle', be prepared for painfully slow signal on wireless dongles as every fan in the stadium gets on the phone network to relay the game, text their mates or update their own Twitter account.

Public relations

Sports public relations (PR) is one of the fastest growing media sectors. Not many years ago, for all but the top teams, the job of looking after the press was done by a club official without specialist training, perhaps with a media background but often not. Now all major teams and associations employ in-house or outsource to PR agencies the job of dealing with all media enquiries, from requests for accreditation to attend events or cover games to access to players or athletes and coaching staff. They will issue press releases, compile media guides at the start of seasons or championships and issue updates on injuries, transfers and other club matters.

Most top teams also have their own in-house journalists, who often get privileged access. They are responsible for everything from the match-day programme to magazines and official websites, which in turn have become additional revenue sources for the clubs. There is often frustration about the practice of using these official channels to break news about the club, presenting it in a positive way. The clubs say that fans are getting the information direct from the source, while reporters counter this by saying it could lead to manipulation of the media. Manchester United was among the first, many have now followed, to have their own television station called MUTV.

United players sign contracts that require them to be interviewed on MUTV and former captain Roy Keane didn't hold back after his side had suffered a surprise 4–1 defeat at Middlesbrough. His opinions were so explosive that the channel decided they couldn't be aired. Any other media outlet would have rightly hailed such an interview as a major scoop but official media's job is to tell the story the club want the fans to hear, which is not always the story the fans want to hear.

The press tribune and media room can often lead to isolation from the fans, so it is worth checking out what they are saying in one of media's big growth areas – citizen journalism. Fanzines and unofficial websites will give you a good flavour of the mood of terraces, although don't misread the thoughts of a vocal few. It is not always the case that they are representing the silent majority.

Statistics

Even though more and more statistical information is going online, most major sports still produce a number of annual yearbooks, which are an invaluable source of records and statistics. Since 1970 – under various sponsors – an annual *Football Yearbook* has been published, containing statistical information on the previous season in English football, including all results, appearances, goalscorers and transfers for the Premier League, Football League, Conference National, Scottish Premier League and Scottish Football League, as well as selected historical records for each club and all major competitions. For more than a century *Wisden*, the hardback, bright-yellow cricketers' almanac, has been essential reading for cricket journalists, while the small more compact *Playfair Annual* is equally stat packed.

Major sports tournaments, such as the Association of Tennis Professionals (ATP) and Women's Tennis Association (WTA) tours and all major golf tours, produce annual media guides that include biographical information about every player. However, this soon becomes outdated and most journalists prefer to use the official website for reference. Reporters covering the Olympics refer to David Wallechinsky's *Complete Book of the Olympics* as their bible. It includes the top-eight finishers in every Olympics held and full descriptions and scoring for every event at the Games. But at nearly 1200 pages, it's much heavier than most laptops.

Most leagues commission regular email bulletins to subscriber journalists to assist with their reporting. The English Premier League produces a weekly email – also available in printed form at grounds – which provides journalists with recent results, historical results between competing sides and a huge range of statistical information, sourced by organisations such as Opta and the Press Association.

The sheer number of betting markets and advent of coaching software such as Prozone has made football a much more statistical sport than ever before – but be careful not to make your coverage read like a maths paper. It is all too easy to punctuate every sentence with a stat – 'that was his first headed goal in 10 matches', 'he has failed to score in the first half all season' or 'he has not kept this many clean sheets in six years'. A well-placed statistic can add emphasis but too many look cluttered.

The rise of Twitter

In just a few short years, Twitter has become the most vital reference tool for journalists and more and more stories are being directly sourced from the website, with athletes often unaware that what they publish is being examined in detail. Australian swimmer Stephanie Rice, winner of three Olympic gold medals, lost a lucrative sponsorship deal after posting a homophobic slur on her Twitter page that was picked up within minutes by the media. England cricketers Kevin Pietersen and Dimitri Mascarenhas were both fined for venting their frustration about selections on Twitter, while Australian batsman Philip Hughes revealed he'd been dropped from an Ashes Test, ahead of an official announcement from the team. Footballers have been known to vent their frustration with transfers and tactics on the social networking site. Former England striker Michael Owen and top golfer Rory McIlroy have even got into exchanges of angry tweets with journalists – all good copy for the following day's papers.

Some sportsmen without the profile – suddenly catapulted into the limelight – can live to regret what they post online. Imogen Bankier and Jenny Wallwork were two British badminton players – with relatively small followings – who became embroiled in a testy Twitter exchange as they both battled to be selected for the London 2012 Olympics. One of their followers was a journalist and the story duly dominated the build-up to the Games and the public's perception of both players. When Great Britain launched its London 2012 Olympic kit, three-times cycling gold medallist Bradley Wiggins was quick to tweet that he wasn't impressed. 'Oh dear! The Olympic kit,' he wrote. The post was removed after less than 20 minutes. Wiggins was perhaps reminded that kit designers Adidas were major sponsors of his cycling team but the damage had been done.

Journalists get frustrated that athletes and players are now so well media managed that they hardly say anything of note when interviewed which is the reason that characters like Ian Holloway and Harry Redknapp are so revered for speaking their mind, even when it lands them in trouble. But Twitter remains a place where indiscretions regularly occur. Keen policing of the accounts is needed to make sure they are verified, as at the last count there were 10 accounts claiming to be the 'real' Lionel Messi. This policing will pay dividends, even if 99.9 per cent is of little interest.

It can also add vital colour to reports. British tennis number one Andy Murray extensively tweets about his off-court life during Wimbledon – which, when you have acres of space, can be a godsend to a tennis press pack.

Andy Murray chose a horror movie for light entertainment on the eve of his second-round match against Tobias Kamke.

The great British hope for the Wimbledon title watched *Scream* to take his mind off the pressure that builds on him every day he progresses deeper into the tournament.

It looked like he got all the fright out of his system because yesterday evening he played like a dream to dispatch the German and move effortlessly into the third round.

Mirror

Andy Murray had a right old *Scream* at Wimbledon – after warming up with a horror flick.

The British No. 1 spent his day off on Tuesday chilling in front of the cult scary movie.

But there were no nightmares on Court No. 1 yesterday, as the world No. 4 saw off German Tobias Kamke 6–3 6–3 7–5 to power through to a third-round date with Croatia's Ivan Ljubicic.

Sun

It also pays to have a scan at the Twitter accounts of athletes before you interview them, perhaps as a conversation starter. For example: 'I saw on Twitter that you've just come back from holiday. Didn't have much luck with the weather did you?' On the flip side, Twitter can be used as an official filter by athletes – who often distrust the media for twisting their words and frequently accuse them of misquoting. Sometimes they have but more often they just did not like how their words appeared in black and white. And when access is being more and more carefully controlled, journalists are simply forced to revise and regurgitate. When Fabio Capello resigned as England football manager in 2012, the only reaction most newspapers and websites carried was from the official Twitter accounts of his players because reporters were denied the chance of asking questions.

Cultivating contacts

Old-school journalists might scoff, perhaps rightly so, at reporters who spend their days surfing websites in search of a story, believing that time would be better spent developing contacts who are willing to speak on or off the record about athletes/players, coaches or officials. These contacts can be developed with teams, or with sporting organisations, from national to international governing bodies and funding agencies. Cultivating contacts is based on trust and takes time. Reporters may often prepare for assignments by ringing trusted sources to get an inside line on preparations for the event or background colour they can use in their reports. Research skills aren't just important in preparing to cover an event or attend an interview. When previewing a major event or upcoming match or laying out a developing story, editors like to break up text with fact boxes or fact files. These contain information and colour that couldn't be included in the main report or that complements it. Sometimes these extra facts are presented in a timeline form – for example, chronicling a particular individual's career – or they could be displayed in bullet points.

When famously reclusive Indian cricketer Sachin Tendulkar finally achieved his 100th first-class century, profile pieces were punctuated with sidebars on his achievements. One such breakout was entitled 'Ten things you didn't know about Tendulkar' and referenced a soon-to-be-published biography of the batsman by Indian cricket writer Gautam Bhattacharya. It included entries like:

> Tendulkar was introduced to the Indian team as a schoolboy by the man he supplanted as India's greatest batsman, Sunil Gavaskar, after acting as a ball boy during Gavaskar's last international innings.

And:

> For much of his career Tendulkar has grown stubble ahead of important matches – 'It's just normal, nothing to do with performance.'

These fact files are compiled through a mixture of research and inside knowledge but be careful where you take your information from, especially online. It can be a 'web of lies' out there. In November 1999, several British newspapers were duped into running stories that Liverpool were about to buy French 'star' Didier Baptiste for £3.5 million. The story had been invented as a joke by an Arsenal fan site and Baptiste didn't exist. Indeed, he was a character on a television programme about a fictitious football club. A journalist spotted this information and wrote it without a cursory check about its validity, paying the price with a very red face.

When Vancouver Canucks winger Rick Rypien tragically took his own life, a Canadian paper was forced to make an apology for what they labelled an 'egregious error' in the report about his death. Their journalist, pressed on a deadline, had lifted a quote from Rypien's Wikipedia entry in which Canucks general manager Mike Gillis had referred to him as 'crazy'. However, Gillis had never made such a comment. It had simply been inserted by one of Wikipedia's public editors. Always remember that Wikipedia is an online encyclopedia – billed as the world's largest reference library – that anyone can edit. The reporter certainly learned the lesson of failing to verify the accuracy of information with proper due diligence. User-generated digital sources should never be used as authoritative sources of information and should never be used as sole sources. It's worth noting that even Wikipedia warns users: 'We do not expect you to trust us.'

Jo Carter, who graduated from her fast-track NCTJ qualification at News Associates three years ago and now works as a deputy editor at ESPN, says:

> Everything on the internet should be double-checked. Even the most trusted sites make mistakes. Wikipedia has a reputation but it's fine as long as you double or triple-check the information on there. Most journalists will use it under caution because of the depth and breadth of information it has. And it always comes near the top of internet searches.

EXERCISE 1

Think of an upcoming sports event or eagerly anticipated match and prepare a breakout fact file-style piece. Do this against the clock. You should be able to cover this comfortably in 30 minutes but bring the deadline forward as you get more experienced. But remember that old journalism adage that making it fast doesn't mean much if you don't make it right.

Include the following information:

- One to watch – someone you expect to stand out.
- Did you know? – find an interesting fact about the match that could surprise readers; for example, 'When the Blues played United in 1971 the game was held up for 10 minutes when a dog ran on to the pitch and refused to leave.'
- Head to head – two individuals, maybe players or coaches, who have a rivalry or interesting history of close or controversial competition
- Odds-on – look at the betting markets and pick up a tip for the game but back it up with some facts; for example, 'The last three matches between these sides at this ground have generated just three goals' or 'United's poor home form but relatively resolute defence, makes 1–0 to City at 4–1 look tempting.'
- Stat attack – sport generates hundreds of statistics and sports fans love talking about them. Use the information available to produce a 50–60 word 'stat attack' on the upcoming event. For example: 'City come into this match on the back of a five-game unbeaten run, with two away victories in the past fortnight. Top scorer Paul Smith, with 17 this season, netted a hat-trick in these teams' last encounter, which will be best remembered for two late red cards for United defenders Joe Jones and Sam Green.'

5

THE BIG MATCH

THE EVOLVING NATURE OF THE MATCH REPORT AND GAME-DAY STORY

How on earth do sportswriters do it? Do they write most of their football/cricket/tennis report while the action is going on, and then go back and write the intro when they know what the result is? Or do they wait till it's all over to start writing? Or do they guess what the result is going to be, write straight through, and then hastily rewrite when a two-footed tackle and a controversial sending-off turn the whole thing upside down in the last five minutes (which they certainly would in tennis)? Nobody's ever told me.

Giles Coren, restaurant critic at The Times

You've got your parking space, nice and close to the entrance, you've been handed your press pass that gives you access to almost all areas, you're enjoying a cup of tea in the media lounge but passed on the sandwiches and now you're sitting in your prime seat, not too high, just on the halfway line, ready for the action to start. Welcome to the pampered, privileged world of the sports journalist. If only it were really always – or even ever – true.

Covering sports is a constant battle with your wits and the clock. People love sport because it's unscripted drama, with ever-changing plot lines. However, when your order is 750 words 'on the whistle' – that means filing your copy as soon as the referee blows for full time or a winning shot is hit – that is guaranteed to lead to frayed nerves. The demands of the internet also add increased pressure on reporters. Now, your requirements might be as follows:

- For your website, file a quick scene-setter before the game – what's the latest team news? Did the manager say anything newsworthy in the match-day programme? Why has that key player been left out again? Does it mean he's off in the summer?

- The desk want to get a story online ASAP and have asked for running copy, also known as a runner, in which the reporter files their words in a series of takes.
- They need 750 words in total and want 400 at half time, 300 with 15 minutes to go and a 50-word intro as soon as it finishes. They'll piece it together back in the office and because the game is on television, they will dress in any good first reaction quotes off the television.
- Don't forget to update your Twitter account but remember, league regulations allow you to do this only every 10 minutes.
- You also might have to revise your runner with another freshened-up piece 20 minutes after the whistle – less kick by kick but more analytical, throwing the story forward if possible for the first edition of the paper. At just 500 words, you can trim it back a bit.

You hope that you can get online to file, if the Wi-Fi stands up or your wireless dongle works. If not, you'll be reading it through to a copytaker and that will really slow you down. Now dash down to the media lounge for both managers' news conference, they are obliged to attend by league rules but they don't always. When you need them quickly, they will invariably spend ages in the dressing-room before arriving and when you are late getting across your match action, they will be there almost as soon as they walk down the tunnel. In that case, you'll have to beg for quotes; remember to be a good guy in the reverse because what goes around comes around.

Now take the quotes and dress them into a revised match report for later editions of tomorrow's paper. Put less focus on the match action and more on moving the story forward and post-game reaction. The desk also wants a quotes-lead sidebar for the back page with a top-newsy angle of the game – only 250 words and they need it in 10 minutes.

Other reporters might have additional requirements, grabbing a player for a future story, trying to gain a couple of additional lines out of a coach or manager that can be used in an upcoming match preview. Increasingly reporters will contribute opinion pieces or blogs to their website as well. It can be stressful but it can also be an incredible adrenaline rush. And if you like to work quietly, remember the sports journalist's office is right in the middle of a packed and noisy stadium and when you're trying to concentrate you can be guaranteed the public address announcer will crank up the music and assault your eardrums. Some press boxes are also situated in the middle of fans, so expect a few friendly suggestions about what you should write.

Jonathan Northcroft, the football correspondent of the *Sunday Times*, has three tips for match reporting:

Firstly, keep calm under pressure, you'll get there. You've done it before or, if it's your first time, hundreds of other journalists, probably a lot worse than you, have managed it and you can too.

Secondly, always hit the deadline: better to file copy you're not entirely happy with than file some award-winning prose that arrives too late to go in the paper!

Finally, work to a formula: whatever one works for you. Mine is 'half the word count at half time; another quarter at 75 minutes, the rest on the whistle'. I nearly always start the first half copy with something significant from the team news/tactical line-ups and in this first chunk of copy I try and describe the general flow of the game (if one side is counterattacking for example), as well as specific incidents. The copy at 75 minutes is functional: more match detail, but it will go at the end of the article so I do try and ensure the last sentence is a plausible one on which a match report can end. The 'top' of the piece is filed on the whistle and I like to try and include the winning goal in this intro part, so I'll save it from the rest of the copy to be used here (though if it's an early goal it'll be in my first half copy and I'll merely refer to it rather than give a full description in the intro). Others have different ways of approaching it but every good journo has a formula.

Included in my principles is one of leaving myself room to be spontaneous – I don't like pre-written match report copy and I don't like preconceived intros. I leave myself a blank page and try to come up with it all on the spot.

More and more sports coverage

In the past, fans may have got their first news of a sports result from their morning newspapers – not any more. There is more live sport on television or online than ever before. Goals from every football game played on a Saturday are broadcast before Sunday morning. Many of the games are live, reports on websites are instantaneous and there are minute-by-minute blogs of the action and Twitter hashtags for fan reactions. In addition, games not broadcast live are later shown 'as live' and even if the game is not on television there are countless websites contravening all the rules of copyright and streaming the action.

Analysis of the game starts at the final whistle and continues online, on radio and on television. By the time readers open their newspapers the following morning, they are probably as well informed about the incidents in the match as the reporter, even if they didn't attend. People now expect what they read in newspapers to give them a different angle. They want analysis and reaction – there's no point describing in detail a controversial red card they've already seen. They want to know what the manager said about it. Was he fuming with the player or the referee?

The above is presented as if the journalist was providing a balanced account of the action but, of course, you might only attend a match or event with a particular interest in one team or athlete. You also need to throw the story forward. There's always the next match, the next round, the next race, or the next season. There are always a story to be pursued and a subplot behind the result to be explored. If all the above seems a little daunting remember that your first assignment is unlikely to be quite so demanding. Perhaps it will be attending a lower-league sporting event, such as a semi-professional football match, and writing just one match report. And your deadline will probably be generous – an hour, perhaps longer, or even the morning after the match. However, if you start learning to write reports 'on the whistle' – sports journalism thrives on speed and accuracy – then that can only help when you've got more time to be more considered. There is plenty of football on television for practice and some suggested example exercises are included in this chapter.

The first key factor for any live report is preparation. Do your research, have information at hand to cover all eventualities. Not everything is a classic and covering your bases in advance can pay dividends if little noteworthy occurs. Arrive in plenty of time. It's better to be at the ground with nothing to do than stressing in your car or on public transport that you might not make it. If you are there for the first time, take a walk to establish the lie of the land. Depending on the status of the club or the event, press facilities can vary. Some might just have a few seats reserved for journalists, others might have a sophisticated media centre.

If you have an immediate deadline – which will involve filing your report from the venue – arrive early to test that everything works, although don't expect it to do so when it really matters.

Copytakers: a dying breed

In the not-too-distant past, most sports reporters rang through their stories to copytakers, who then forwarded them straight to the copy baskets of the relevant editors. These super-fast typists could take in a 500-word report in just a few minutes, although all names needed to be spelled out letter by letter, so if you were covering an Everton match you would hope that Diniyar Bilyaletdinov would be anonymous. Financial reality and the ease of instant communication means copytakers, sadly, are being phased out of journalism, going the way of the hot-metal press. It's a shame because they have often been blamed for some of the most amusing sports-page gaffes – although most were caught by subeditors before they made it into print. In a cricket report, a batsman returned to a ground where he'd had previous success and the reporter's phrase 'self-same arena' became 'Selsey Marina' while 'Liverpool duly presented Norwich with goals' in a football match report was interpreted as 'Liverpool Julie presented Norwich with girls'. There's also a famous story about a report from a Welsh football international in which the correspondent's sentence about 'the attack being led by Rush and Hughes' became 'the attack being led by Russian Jews'.

It is now expected that most journalists will file from their laptops – so while they now have no one to blame for typographical errors (typos), it gives them more time to craft their reports, watch the action and not have to worry about making phone calls. However, wireless internet devices cannot be relied on. Some events take place in remote areas, such as finishes to cycle races, and Wi-Fi can easily fall over when every reporter hits 'send' and every photographer starts sending through their images. For this reason, major events such as the Olympics now provide cabled internet access for stability, although this can carry a hefty usage charge. Getting to the ground early allows you time to familiarise yourself with the internet facilities. It doesn't matter how good your report is if you can't file it. One trick, because phone signals often jam up as soon as a match or event finishes, is to press 'send' on your story just a few minutes before it concludes – with a note that says the match is still in progress. If a late incident occurs, you can always ring and amend your copy – but at least the desk will have it.

Also remember to think of practicalities. Charge your laptop and your phone. Nothing irritates a desk more than not being able to contact its 'eyes' on the scene. Take an extension lead too because power points can be in short supply. Don't rely on there being a clock so have a stopwatch. Take more than one pen.

In addition, take time to establish the protocol for getting quotes after a game, with press officers the best point of reference. Many US sports operate an open locker-room policy after and even before the matches but this does not happen in the UK and Europe. You might need to grab athletes, players or coaches as they exit the field of play – they might gather a gaggle of journalists around them outside the dressing-room or attend an organised press conference. You might have to collar them in the car park on the way to their bus or cars. Of course, if you already have strong contacts with a team, in a sport or with an individual, you may be able to call them to get their reaction – if your deadline permits.

In the mixed zone

Gathering quotes directly after an event can work two ways. Either interviewees are on a high or low and will say something that, after a period of reflection, they may not have. Alternatively, and this is more often the case, they are too tired or too media trained to say anything newsworthy. Bland, vanilla quotes crammed with clichés soon turn readers off. At some major events, such as the Olympic Games or World Athletics Championships, athletes must pass through an area known as a mixed zone, although they are not obliged to stop. Host broadcasters and rights-holding television companies have priority positions, followed by radio and written press. It took British diver Tom Daley more than an hour to pass through the mixed zone at the Beijing Olympics in 2008 and he didn't even win a medal. At the World Cup, players pass through the mixed zone as they head from the dressing-room to their bus. Usually it's agreed in advance with team media officials which players might stop. Sometimes certain players are assigned specific media categories: player A for daily newspapers, player B for evening newspapers and player C for Sunday newspapers. David McDonnell of the *Daily Mirror* wrote amusingly about his experiences trying to get quotes in a mixed zone during the 2010 FIFA World Cup in South Africa:

> Pulling a player in a World Cup mixed zone for interview is like trying to catch the eye of a beautiful woman in a bar. Chances are she'll not even acknowledge your presence. And even if she does, she's likely to look straight through you with a withering, contemptuous look that says 'as if'. It's a soul-destroying, dignity-stripping exercise at times, being snubbed by footballers affronted at the temerity of journalists wanting to ask for their views on the game in which they have just played. English players – with a few notable exceptions – are among the worst culprits, striding past waiting reporters with such disdain you can almost smell it above the whiff of expensive fragrance they douse themselves in after games.

Some sports, like golf and tennis, organise press conferences – and also helpfully provide verbatim transcripts within minutes, which is both helpful for journalists and ensures no one is misquoted. Court stenographers bash away at 300 words per minute – most reporters have 100 words per minute shorthand – and their keyboard connects via Bluetooth to a nearby laptop, where an assistant checks for mistakes. After a typical interview, the transcript is emailed to on-site reporters, who have opted in, or distributed in paper copy. It's particularly helpful when lots of interviews are happening back to back and allows reporters the chance to stay in the loop even when they haven't attended the press conference. According to Chris Hewitt, who graduated from journalism college two years ago and now works for the *Watford Observer*:

> Preparation is key. I've always got lots of statistics available to put the game into context – a team's run of form, goal tallies for individual players, head-to-head results etc. They help enormously when you are under pressure and quickly tapping out a couple of paragraphs about the action.
>
> Write as you go but don't go mad. I type up the key events – goals, near misses, penalty appeals as they happen but people don't need to read every last detail. It's hard but don't get so absorbed in note taking that you don't watch any of the game.

Now you've done all your preparation work, you are ready for the action to start. Let's imagine we are covering a football match and we've been asked to file 500 words 'on the whistle'. When you are filing 'on the whistle' – a term that can equally apply to a tennis match or golf tournament – you have to construct your report as the action is ongoing. You can't wait until the last few minutes and then bash out the words; that way you are going to miss the deadline.

As a reporter in the field, your focus is rightly entirely on your assignment but it's important to think of your editors back in the office. On a busy Saturday afternoon, UK sports press agency Sportsbeat has reporters at more than 200 football matches and 100 rugby union matches – and that's before you add in those filing from an athletics meeting or cycle race. Those editors worry about the whole picture. Some reporters might have high-profile assignments but they are cogs in a big wheel. If one deadline gets missed, it can hold up the entire operation – no excuse, from laptop failure to lack of phone signal, is going to be accepted. David Parsons, Sportsbeat's executive editor says:

> With so much going on a Saturday, my focus remains on the top-line stories from the day and making sure all our commitments – from web stories to camera-ready pages for newspapers – are fulfilled. The reporter will be notified by email of their order, for example 300 words 'on the whistle' and a 450-word quotes rewrite, with reaction from both managers. We might

also want some statistics such as player ratings, substitutions, times, and match and referee ratings. We give them a deadline and ask them to file by email. Some news desks do – but we don't – ask for reporters to call in to make sure their copy has arrived, known as a 'check call'. Otherwise, we'd need three staff just to answer phones for our busiest period.

Instead, we ask them to stay on standby until a certain time, usually 45 minutes after their final deadline, so we can go back to them if their copy has not arrived or the designated subeditor has any queries. We want self-sufficient reporters. We are monitoring all games and if we need something we will call but use your initiative.

However, they must remember we are relying on them. We follow all matches closely but it's possible a newsworthy incident might get missed and such an incident might change our news agenda, promoting the story from a few paragraphs to a page lead. For example, one of our reporters was covering a semi-professional match interrupted by a streaker. Nothing out of the ordinary there, exhibitionists of this sort are hardly newsworthy and our general rule is avoid them to deny them the oxygen of publicity. However, in this match the manager of one team snapped. He ran on to the pitch and hauled the intruder to the ground. The referee reacted by sending the manager off. In the melee that ensured, two of his coaching staff went and two of his players. Thankfully, the reporter on the scene realised this was a good story and immediately alerted us. We were able to dedicate more space to it as a result. If that reporter had just filed it as part of his match report, we'd have lost critical time and might not have been able to do the story justice.

Each reporter will have a different way of tackling an 'on the whistle' story. Some might watch the first half and then use the relative peace and quiet of half time to start compiling their report. It's said that an ideal football match to cover would feature loads of first-half incidents and a second half in which little of note occurs – unfortunately these are rare. Statistics prove that more goals are scored in the second half of football matches than in the first, especially in the last 10 minutes as players become tired.

Imagine covering the 1999 Champions League Final and writing an 'on the whistle' report. With injury time being added, Manchester United were behind to Bayern Munich's sixth-minute goal, scored by Mario Basler. The reporters will have written their stories – focusing on the heartache for United boss Sir Alex Ferguson as the dreams of an unprecedented treble are dashed, after the side had already won the Premier League title and FA Cup Final. Then, one minute into added time, Teddy Sheringham equalised. Cue frantic rewriting but the game was surely now heading towards 30 minutes of extra time, easing the deadline pressure. However, Ole Gunnar Solskjær then popped up to grab United's improbable winner just two minutes later with virtually the last kick of the game. And the report was still needed as soon as the whistle blew.

Six years later, many of the reporters who earned their stripes that night were back for the final between Milan and Liverpool. At half time, their stories would have been written, with Milan stunning Liverpool with three goals. Within 15 minutes of the restart though, the score was 3–3 and the match was decided on penalties. If you were writing an 800-word match report that night, you probably wrote over 4000 words during the course of the match, with the delete key getting the heaviest treatment.

So the key is to prepare for any eventuality and use all available tools to give yourself an advantage. For example, if the match you were attending was being broadcast on radio, you might choose to listen to the commentary while you reported, because it could give you another perspective. It could also assist with any action you missed. It's amazing how little of the game you watch in the closing minutes if you are producing an 'on the whistle' report. Some events provide television in press boxes and media tribunes, giving reporters in attendance the benefit of action replays – which can be so critical if there has been a contentious event.

If writing 500 words, you could adopt the following strategy. Aim to have 300 words written by the end of the first half, words on the screen are valuable, especially if the second half is less noteworthy. Make a call on your intro with about 10 minutes to go. If the score is 3–1 another goal will probably not change what you've written, the winning time's margin will either be even more comfortable or just a little closer. And don't be worried about a late and decisive goal – there can be no arguments about this being the right angle to lead on if it occurs.

Writing the first two paragraphs

The first two paragraphs of a match report remain the most important – they should draw readers in and make them want to read on. Ideally, it's lead on a name and the intro should throw itself forward. Look at these examples of a first paragraph, under the heading 'Manchester United 1 Liverpool 0' – which do you think is best?

1   Manchester United boosted their title chances as they beat arch-rivals Liverpool 1–0 at Old Trafford.

Wayne Rooney scored his seventh goal in four games but left it late, heading past Pepe Reina in the 89th minute.

2   Wayne Rooney scored a late goal as Manchester United boosted their title chances against arch-rivals Liverpool.

Rooney's 89th-minute header, his seventh goal in four games, left Pepe Reina flat-footed and heaped pressure on under-fire Anfield manager Kenny Dalglish.

3   Wayne Rooney continued his red-hot scoring form as Manchester United boosted their title hopes and heaped more pressure on Liverpool manager Kenny Dalglish.

It was Rooney's seventh goal in four games and while he left it late, scoring with an 89th-minute header, it was the most valuable yet.

The first intro does little more than repeat the scoreline and tell you something a well-informed football fan would already know, which is that Liverpool and Manchester United are rivals and the latter plays at Old Trafford. It tells readers nothing they couldn't have learned just by seeing the result. The second intro starts to add in a little more colour, while the third intro adds colour and context.

'On the whistle' reports should not be chronological, just presenting the match information as it happens. Sports reporting isn't like reading a murder mystery, when you find out that the butler committed the crime on the final page. The most newsworthy material from the event should be covered right at the top of your copy. In an ideal world, the first four paragraphs of the report should sum up the entire game; the rest can add depth and context, which is easier to cut should the space allocated to your report be reduced.

Keep the paragraphs short and snappy – you need to go beyond purely describing the action. Remember that the audience for your piece is the audience that attended your event. Try to help them understand why, rather than tell them what. You can do this by judicious use of statistical information, gained from research. For example, which of the below sounds more authoritative to the readers?

Murray took less than two hours to beat Cipolla and will now face Japan's Tatsuma Ito in the second round.

Murray continued his 10-match unbeaten streak as he took less than two hours to beat Cipolla and will now face Japan's Tatsuma Ito in the second round.

Murray continued his 10-match unbeaten streak as he took less than two hours to beat Cipolla and will now face Japan's Tatsuma Ito, a player he confidently beat in their only previous encounter, in the second round.

Computers: the new rivals?

If a player has been sent off, prior research can add depth and colour, for example, 'Djibril Cissé saw red for a rash 63rd-minute challenge', does not sounds as good as, 'Djibril Cissé's rash 63rd-minute challenge caused him to see red for the second time in five matches.' However, reports need more than just description of action and statistics, such is the evolving nature of sports journalism. Because your rivals now aren't just others who sit alongside you in the press box but computers, churning out robotic, almost lifeless journalism. Recently students at Northwestern University in the United States developed a computer programme that took statistics and scores from a baseball match, admittedly one of the most stat-heavy sports, and automatically generated a match report the moment the game concluded. The programme includes a library of commonly used narratives in sports reporting and replaces the journalist's news judgement with a computer algorithm. The worse thing is that the report wasn't that bad. See the report below, generated without human involvement. Bear in mind that this is the very baseline standard for your reporting and also that this technology is only going to get better.

Things looked bleak for the Angels when they trailed by two runs in the ninth inning, but Los Angeles recovered thanks to a key single from Vladimir Guerrero to pull out a 7–6 victory over the Boston Red Sox at Fenway Park on Sunday. Guerrero drove in two Angels runners. He went 2–4 at the plate. Guerrero has been good at the plate all season, especially in day games. During day games Guerrero has a .794 OPS. He has hit five home runs and driven in 13 runners in 26 games in day games. After Chone Figgins walked, Bobby Abreu doubled and Torii Hunter was intentionally walked, the Angels were leading by one when Guerrero came to the plate against Jonathan Papelbon with two outs and the bases loaded in the ninth inning. He singled scoring Abreu from second and Figgins from third, which gave Angels the lead for good. Angels starter Scott Kazmir struggled, allowing five runs in six innings, but the bullpen allowed only one run and the offense banged out 11 hits to pick up the slack and secure the victory for the Angels. J.D. Drew drove in two Red Sox runners. He went 1–4 at the plate. Drew homered in the fourth inning scoring Mike Lowell. Drew has been excellent at the plate all season, especially in day games. During day games Drew has a .914 OPS. He has hit five home runs and driven in 17 runners in 36 games in day games. Papelbon blew the game for Boston with a blown save. Papelbon allowed three runs on four hits in one inning. Reliever Darren Oliver got the win for Los Angeles. He allowed no runs over one-third of an inning. The Los Angeles lefty struck out none, walked none and surrendered no hits. Los Angeles closer Brian Fuentes got the final three outs to record the save. Juan Rivera and Kendry Morales helped lead the Angels. They combined for three hits, three RBIs and one run scored. Four relief pitchers finished off the game for Los Angeles. Jason Bulger faced four batters in relief out of the bullpen, while Kevin Jepsen managed to record two outs to aid the victory.

It's hardly going to win you an award but, unfortunately, there is a lot worse on the internet and published in newspapers. However, it takes experience to be able to produce match reporting that reads more like literary non-fiction, lengthy, sometimes poetic with well-executed digressions into backstory. When done well this sort of reporting is the reason why the best writing in any branch of journalism can be found in the sports section. When done badly, it can miss the mark by a mile, so don't overreach when you are starting out. But remember your key role is to inform, not just regurgitate information. Match reports should add to the conversation and, increasingly, there is room for well-placed opinion, backed up by fact.

In today's digital age, there is still a place for the instant match report, although it could be argued the 'game story' – published hours or even days after the event – is becoming more and more irrelevant for newspapers with increasing competition from television, the internet and social media. In the UK, national reporters still cover matches on Saturday afternoon for papers that won't be published until Monday morning, while locally a weekly title might not publish a review of match information until days after the event has concluded.

The internet has made it easy to access information. The fan experience doesn't stop and finish at the turnstile, it continues after the match on Twitter, Facebook and YouTube. Journalists should realise, as circulations shrink, that they need to be part of this conversation, hence the reason many are building a large Twitter audience, with ESPN's National Football League reporter Adam Schefter often breaking news first to his one million followers, which in turn drives them to the more in-depth content he creates. Henry Winter, the award-winning football correspondent of the *Daily Telegraph*, also now makes time every day to answer messages sent to him by his 400,000-plus followers.

Internet sites demand quick and accurate copy – underlining that old journalism mantra about making it 'fast, first and right' – but match reports in newspapers, and those who write them, need to adapt. The tried and tested formula for their production, used for decades, is becoming as tired as some of the prose used. Newspapers no longer enjoy a monopoly over reporting events in an age when every fan with a Twitter account is reacting to and breaking news, the world has become a publisher and incurred no expense in the process. However, it should not be seen as all doom and gloom. The best journalists still find a way to tell their readers something they didn't know – using their own contacts and experience – well after an event has concluded. Rather it's gossip from behind the scenes, an informed observation that escaped much public debate, a news story or a well-turned phrase or just plain good writing, honed with practice and experience.

Moments after Linford Christie won his Olympic 100m gold in 1992, the wires – the forerunner of today's internet – crackled with the intro:

Great Britain's Linford Christie stormed to 100m gold to become, at 32, the oldest ever winner of the blue-riband Olympic event.

You can't fault it for informing the reader promptly and accurately and while the below – written in the pages of the *Daily Mail* by the peerless sportswriter Ian Wooldridge – doesn't add much more detail, it was still worth waiting the extra few hours for.

There are two ways to get your own back on a stifling summer's night. One is to go out and beat up an inner city. Another is to go to the Olympic Games and smash the world in the 100 metres. Thank God that Linford Christie chose the other.

It is no secret that as a young black man from the Caribbean he did not find London's streets paved with equality. Hopefully his riposte will prove inspirational to others who feel similarly crushed. It was a run powered as much by maniacal determination as muscle and finely tuned technique.

Award-winning journalist of the *Racing Post*, Lee Mottershead says:

If I'm writing a big-race report I know that the readers will know everything that happened in the race by the time they pick up their newspaper. My job is not so much to tell them what happened but to expand their knowledge and understanding of the event while also entertaining them. *Racing Post* major reports are written in a colourful, descriptive style for that reason. Online you get the initial first take on the race but in the newspaper readers should get a crafted piece of writing, something with a beginning, middle and end, something that flows seamlessly for pace and rhythm. Always aim high.

Match reporting is a bit like taking up golf. The first time you play at a golf course you shoot 140 and lose a bag of balls. But you make quick improvements by playing regularly. With practice, it is possible to go from bad to average quite quickly, although getting to good, great and world-class takes a bit more hard work. And the same applies to match reporting.

With the proliferation of football on television, you can constantly be practising your match reporting skills. Do your research before the game, print out the team sheets and then set yourself different tasks. Perhaps attempt a runner with different takes during the game and vary your word count on the final whistle. Set yourself a deadline and stick to it. Then take a break, read through your copy and see what you would correct because errors get made when you are under pressure. Always write to your deadline. If copy has been requested for 5 p.m., file it then. There's always a sentence to be improved and an angle to be polished.

Finally, you'll need to known the things to avoid. There is too much hype in sports journalism. Why does every shot have to be slammed and why does every tackle have to be crunching? Emotive language is good when used for impact but when overused it looks lazy. Clichés are even worse, no matter how clever you may think they are you can be guaranteed they've been used before and it will make your editor – and those that subedit your work – as sick as a parrot. A personal bugbear of mine is copy that reads more like weather reports. Do fans really need to know that the 'skies were leaden grey and threatening drizzle as Rovers kicked off into a strong headwind'? Unless the weather is making a major impact on your story – strong winds in a golf tournament or wet weather at a motorsport event – it can be avoided. Match reporting, in particular the ability to write 'on the whistle', remains a great skill. If you can produce quality copy against a deadline then other tasks will appear much simpler.

EXERCISE 2

Objectivity is key to journalism but analysis and opinion have a place in sports reporting, provided they are backed up by fact. You might be asked to provide a match report that is 'balanced' in which equal prominence should to be given to both sides. However, if you are writing for a regional title or a national title, in an international situation, reporting will obviously be skewed to one side or individual.

Watch a football match live on television and prepare two reports – both must be provided 10 minutes after the final whistle, so you will be compiling them side by side during the match. Aim to write 250 words for each version. Remember by the time the readers see your story they are likely to have seen the goals or heard about any key incidents. There might be common themes and elements but it is likely the intro and main thrust of each story will be different – one team might be extending their unbeaten run and challenging for promotion, the other might be slumping to their fifth straight defeat and propping up the table. In advance of the game, do your prematch research, print out the teamsheets and relevant statistics – league tables, leading scorers, recent results and head-to-head statistics – as well as prematch team news and manager comments.

EXERCISE 3

From the same match you watched for Exercise 2, give yourself more time to write a 500-word match report that will be published two days later ('day plus two'). You'll have time to see the post-match reaction and monitor the fallout of the game on social media. Aim to throw the story forward, focusing on the fallout and its ramifications for forthcoming matches. Write the story as if it were appearing in the local media of the losing team.

6

HOW TO DO IT

DEALING WITH ROUND-UPS AND PRESS RELEASES

Sports are in competition with other sports every day, competing for space in newspapers and online. There is only so much resource and not every game or tournament can be covered in depth. However, the demand for content remains insatiable and certain publishers have successfully targeted this niche. David Emery, a former *Daily Express* sports editor, has a stable of four national newspaper titles, headed by the *Non-League Paper* and the *Rugby Paper*. The former has been published every Sunday since 2000 and carries match reports from semi-professional games across England and Wales from the Football Conference downwards. The latter covers rugby union in depth – in addition to international games and professional top-flight matches, it has reporters out at amateur games across the country – nearly 100 every weekend. Emery also publishes the *Football Paper*, which focuses on the English professional game outside the Premier League, and the *Cricket Paper*, a midweek publication that covers the sport from the village green to the Test arena. In addition to match reports, all four papers carry extensive round-ups from other leagues and competitions, and carry hundreds of results every week.

Many new arrivals on a sports desk might find themselves asked to provide a round-up – from darts and football to skittles and cricket – it's the best way of condensing large amounts of information into the limited space available. There might be 10 games played in a particular league but no space to carry individual reports, so those 10 reports are edited into a single report. The journalist will then collate the content – the scorers, the match incidents and the impact on the league table – and then try to order the information in the best way possible. There may be a number of sources, including official information such as a press release or website, contributed material or direct contact from the reporter to the clubs involved.

Deciding what the line on the story is remains key. What's the biggest story – the league leaders being held to a draw by a club without a win all season or the second-ranked team beating the third-ranked team to move within a point of the top and extend their unbeaten run to a club record of 10 matches?

There may be a particular noteworthy incident that needs promoting, such as an injury, a sending-off followed by an ugly scuffle between opposing benches or a game being called off because of weather conditions. You must mention all the scores but some games will merit several paragraphs and others no more than a sentence.

Writing a round-up

As an exercise, study the information below from four matches played on the opening day of the women's National Hockey League premier division. Imagine your paper has been provided with four match reports individually, but you've only got space for one 225-word round-up of all action. After reading, compile your report.

Match 1 – Chelmsford 1 Bowdon Hightown 6

Bowdon Hightown, second in last year's National League, began their campaign to go one better with a confident performance against Chelmsford.

The home team Chelmsford, in their first match following promotion, looked out of their depth as the visitors took control after just two minutes.

Becky Towers, in her first match in 18 months, following a succession of cruciate ligament injuries, opened the scoring from a short corner.

British international Emma Price then banked two quick-fire goals in open play while Rebecca John made it 4–0 with a swift breakaway before half time.

Chelmsford reduced arrears shortly after the break with Vanessa Sweet taking advantage after she found herself in acres of space.

Price then added two more to compete the rout and she is now just two goals short of scoring her 300th league goal – a feat that has never previously been achieved.

England international Sarah Smyth missed the match for Chelmsford but is expected to return from a knee injury next week.

Match 2 – Slough 3 Poynton 2

Reigning champions Slough made tough work of their opening fixture of the season.

Coach Henry Watters was forced to make several changes after three key players, including last season's top scorer Danielle Meares, suffered training injuries.

And they soon went behind to Poynton, who broke the deadlock in the 32nd minute after an own goal.

Welsh international Emma John, who started her career at Poynton, crashed a short corner against the post minutes later but made amends with an equaliser just after the break.

Donna Stadlier put Slough in control before Poynton levelled just three minutes from time through Alyson Chiles.

But Poynton coach James Bradman was fuming at a late refereeing decision that awarded Slough a penalty – which John duly converted.

Match 3 – Leicester 3 Olton 0

Olton might have finished last season with 12 straight wins – ensuring a third-place finish – but they came down to earth with a bump against Leicester.

Inspired by Ruth Alder, Leicester, fourth last season, were three goals to the good by half time.

Alder scored them all to underline why she was voted last season's player of the year by her peers.

But the international endured a second half to forget as Great Britain coach Elliott Schurder, watching from the sidelines, was left fuming.

Alder is now a major doubt for next month's Olympic qualifying tournament after clashing with British team-mate Sara Cornwell.

Both players hobbled off leaving Schurder with a real selection headache.

Match 4 – Ipswich 2 Trojans 2

Great Britain's star striker Rosie Brooker was sent off as Trojans were made to pay by Ipswich.

Alix Wright and Brooker put the visitors on course for a seemingly certain victory with goals in the first 20 minutes.

Brooker then fired two consecutive short corners against the post as Trojans ran amok.

Ipswich continued to struggle after the break but Brooker's dismissal turned the match back in their favour.

Claire Sanders, a summer arrival from Clifton, marked her league debut with a cracking shot in the penultimate minute and almost from the restart Teresa Clinton made sure of a share of the spoils.

Across those four reports, you have over 500 words that you need to trim to just 225.

You now need to decide which information you want and which information you don't and in this sort of exercise what you exclude is vital. When you've got a limited word count and lots of information to include then tight writing skills are key – no word should be wasted. There is no room for any repetition. The first step is to break down each individual match report – strip it down to only its key information.

Even if you have no knowledge of the teams and players, it's clear that in the first match Bowdon Hightown are one of the stronger teams in the league; they finished second last year and were confident 6–1 winners over Chelmsford, who have just been promoted. This was a confident win and Rebecca John emerges as the key personality with four goals and she is nearing a milestone mark of 300 career league goals.

In the second match, the key angle appears to be the reigning champions surviving a scare but emerging 3–2 winners. They were without a key player due to injury and there is a nice line about a current player, who also happens to be an international, playing her former club. There is also controversy, the Poynton coach being angry after a controversial late penalty.

Olton and Leicester, who feature in the third match, are clearly top teams, finishing third and fourth in the previous season. Ruth Alder must feature heavily in the report because she scored all three goals and was injured. There is a strong line here about the Great Britain coach being in attendance and Alder, and another player, now expected to be absent from a few forthcoming international tournaments.

The final match was also not without controversy – an international player scoring to put her side, Trojans, two goals up. She was then sent off and with a numerical advantage the hosts scored twice to equalise, with a late goal adding to the drama.

So what would you lead on? The reigning champions surviving a scare? An injury to a star British player ahead of an important Olympic qualifier? A player nearing a record goal total or Britain's star striker being sent off?

> Ruth Alder is a major injury doubt for next month's Olympic qualifying tournament after she was injured in the opening fixture of the National Hockey League.

This is clearly the strongest news line – appealing to the widest audience. The interest in club hockey is relatively small but the international game, in particular the Olympics, is more closely followed.

Great Britain coach Elliott Schurder would have been delighted to see Leicester's Alder, voted last season's player of the year, score three times in the first half of their 3–0 victory over Olton.

Always look to throw stories forward – what is the cause and consequence of the result?

But he was fuming after she collided with British team-mate Sara Cornwell, both players hobbling off to leave Schurder with a real selection headache.

You've committed just over 80 words of your story to one game – no harm done there. You should make sure all games are covered but you don't need to do this equally.

Defending champions Slough survived a scare at home against Poynton before emerging 3–2.

This is probably the second strongest story – a close match involving the defending champions with some late controversy. But the champions didn't lose, they managed to find a way to win the game at a late stage – which is something champions tend to do. Remember it's the first game of the season, there are many games left, and nothing is decided yet.

However, it wasn't until former Poynton player Emma John scored a late penalty, which was fiercely contested by visiting coach James Bradman, that the points were secured.

It's impossible considering the number of words you have available to mention every scorer – across these four games there were 19 goals, so pick out the key incidents and focus on them.

Bowdon Hightown's Emma Price scored four as league newcomers Chelmsford were given a salutary lesson about the task ahead this season after a 6–1 home defeat. Price is now just two goals short of scoring her 300th league goal – a feat that has never previously been achieved.

The third best story – Price clearly scores goals with regularity and the win was pretty one-sided. If Price had scored her milestone goal it might be good lead but she didn't – she still has two more to score.

Elsewhere, Great Britain and Trojans striker Rosie Brooker was sent off as hosts Ipswich staged a battling fightback. Alix Wright and Brooker put the visitors ahead but the latter's dismissal changed the tide of the game and Claire Sanders and Teresa Clinton scored in the closing minutes to secure a share of the spoils.

The fourth best game in terms of news value – with Brooker's dismissal, she is Great Britain's star striker, clearly the best line to emerge from the game. Like match reporting, practising round-ups is quite easy. Perhaps choose a schedule of Premier League games or county cricket matches and produce a round-up within 30 minutes of the final whistle or stumps. Test yourself further by attempting sports less well known to you. For example, produce a round-up of the most relevant action from an afternoon of horse racing, perhaps spread across several meetings. Remember to always throw reports forward and weave in analysis and statistics, so prior research is vital. Vary your deadline as you get more adept at producing the reports and compare and contrast them with what is written online and in newspapers. Did you get the right angle?

EXERCISE 4

You are working a shift on the sports desk of a national press agency. The following copy has been submitted by freelance reporters from games played that day in the Rugby League Challenge Cup, a prestigious knockout competition now at the quarter-final stage. The final will be staged at Wembley. Using the copy below, you are required to write a 200-word round-up for a online client to be published immediately.

Wigan Warriors 43 Harlequins 12
Trent Barrett was in irresistible form as he laid on five tries to help Wigan cruise past Harlequins and into the last four.

The former Australian Test stand-off, 30, was back to his best after a slow start to the season and Quins had no answer to his creativity.

Barrett sent in impressive youngsters Darrell Goulding and Liam Colborn before the break and had a hand in tries for Harrison Hansen, Gareth Hock and Andy Coley in the second half.

The Warriors, who have won the cup 17 times, will now face holders Hull FC in the semi-finals but may have to do without rampaging prop Iafeta Paleaaesina after he was put on report for a high tackle on Quins centre Matt Gafa.

St Helens 23 Widnes Vikings 22

National League One side Widnes Vikings gave 12-man St Helens a huge scare at Knowsley Road before bowing out to a last-minute drop goal from Sean Long.

Reigning 'Man of Steel' James Roby was sent off in the first half for a needless trip on Bob Beswick with the Saints cruising 16–0 up.

Rising stars Matty Smith, Paul Clough and Stephen Tryer had all crossed for Daniel Anderson's men but the Vikings bossed proceedings once Roby saw red five minutes before the break.

Aussie prop Jim Gannon kicked off the visitors fightback before Paul Noone and former Saint Ian Hardman levelled the match.

And Widnes looked set for a famous upset when Beswick went over and Gavin Dodd converted for a 22–16 lead.

But Ade Gardner's converted try cancelled out the advantage before Long kept his cool at the death to land his drop goal from 15 yards and set up a repeat of last year's Super League Grand Final against Leeds.

Leeds Rhinos 32 Huddersfield Giants 8

England captain Jamie Peacock was rushed to hospital after being knocked unconscious during a routine win for Leeds Rhinos.

The rampaging forward was on the wrong end of Eorl Crabtree's swinging forearm and lost consciousness as the Giants prop received a red card from referee Ashley Klein.

Jamahl Lolesi crashed over from close range to give the Giants a dream start but Leeds hit back with Danny McGuire, Rob Burrow and Brent Webb all scoring before the interval.

Captain Kevin Sinfield converted his own try to break Huddersfield's resistance on the hour, the 51st consecutive match he has been on the scoresheet.

Luke Burgess completed the win a minute from time but coach Brian McClellan will be sweating on news about Peacock.

Hull FC 36 Catalan Dragons 16

Hull winger Gareth Raynor eased the pressure on under-fire coach Peter Sharp with a hat-trick to help the holders past plucky Catalan Dragons.

Sections of the KC Stadium crowd had been calling for Sharp's head after a dreadful start to the season but Great Britain star Raynor silenced the critics with a superb display of finishing.

> Thomas Bosc got the French side off to a flier with a second-minute try but Raynor, Danny Washbrook and Gareth Granger gave the Airlie Birds a 20–8 half-time lead.
>
> Raynor then raced 70 metres to extend the lead and completed his hat-trick 12 minutes from time after good work from Adam Dykes.
>
> Dragons captain Gregory Mounis and Aaraon Gorrell brought some respectability to the scoreline in the final five minutes but the damage had already been done.
>
> The draw for the semi-finals has been made – Wigan Warriors will host Hull FC and St Helens will welcome Leeds Rhinos.

Remember the key lessons:

- The most newsworthy line is not always the result, so add in some detail to make it more interesting; for example, 'United moved five points clear', or 'United opened up a gap on their nearest rivals City ahead of next week's local derby with their biggest win of the season'. Prior research is vital to provide the above analysis.
- When working under pressure beware of accuracy, particularly with names. There are some tough spellings in the rugby league reports above. No matter how good a report is, if you make a spelling error on a key individual's name you won't be allowed to forget it.
- Always try to throw your story forward. Fans like to know the cause and consequence of a game, so weave the draw through the copy; for example, 'Wigan will now face defending champions Hull FC in the semi-finals after their confident 36–16 win over Catalan Dragons.'
- Remember when your story is being published. In this case, it's immediately but don't say 'this afternoon' or 'this morning' in the copy. If it's going online it might be read by someone in Australia and his morning might be someone else's evening.

Budgets dictate that editors cannot cover every piece of sporting action that takes place with their own resource. In addition to staff reporters, they will use freelancers or stringers, who specialise in certain sports or cover geographic areas. Editors will also have access to press agencies, who provide a raft of coverage to their clients and official information sent to them by teams and national governing bodies. This information usually takes the form of emailed press releases. Usually, this content is not presented in the right style and will need to be rewritten quickly by a reporter or subeditor based on the news desk.

Lead on a name

Where possible stories should always lead on a name. Sport is about personality, but press releases often don't focus on particular players or athletes because official organisations don't want to be seen to give undue prominence to a particular individual. Much like round-ups, the decision is what to lead on, what to cover and what to omit. In an ideal world, you would always seek to put your own mark on a press release, by making a call, requesting an interview and threading through your own knowledge. For example, an official organisation might issue a release of results from an athletics meeting. They are very unlikely to say that a particular individual has just returned from a drugs ban, but this would be key information that you must add into your story. However, sometimes the demands of deadlines mean, for an initial quick take on the news, you have to work with the press release and the information presented. For example, take this press release issued by British Gymnastics:

European Gymnastics Championships
Brussels (BEL) – British gymnasts enjoyed a successful afternoon on the concluding day in Belgium.

Reigning British all-round champion Hannah Whelan won both the beam and floor bronze medals in an outstanding performance to end the 2012 Women's Artistic Gymnastics European Championships.

Having led the team all week it was her turn to shine as an individual, as she performed a superb beam routine under high pressure to score 14.333 as Romania's Catalina Ponor and Larisa Iordache won gold and silver respectively.

The beam medal is Britain's first ever at a major championships on that piece, and testament to Hannah's great experience and composure under pressure after she fell on the apparatus during the team competition final, where a youthful British team placed fourth.

On floor she produced a perfectly executed routine, with outstanding dance, great confidence, maturity, and plenty of style scoring 14.533; Iordache won gold and Ponor silver.

The Beijing Olympian and reigning British champion claims her first major medals to complete a very encouraging week for the British team in which Gabrielle Jupp also took floor bronze in the junior event, and 15-year-old new seniors Rebecca Tunney and Ruby Harrold both made apparatus finals with outstanding championship performances.

Hannah Whelan: 'It feels amazing. I'm over the moon – it's really unexpected. I wanted to come out and enjoy the competition and I definitely did. I enjoy training beam and feel naturally comfortable on it and to get our first ever medal on that piece is very special. I've always dreamed of getting major medals and to come away with two is unbelievable. It gives me a lot of confidence going into the rest of the year and, hopefully the Olympics.'

From the information above see this 225-word rewritten version:

Hannah Whelan claimed double bronze – including Britain's first-ever major beam medal – at the European Gymnastics Championships in Brussels.

Always try to lead on a name – Hannah was the obvious stand-out gymnast with two bronze medals, including a historic first on the beam, which is a key bit of information that needs prominent inclusion.

Whelan stuttered on the beam during Saturday's team final, in which a youthful British squad finished fourth, but she put that right in style in the individual finals.

Context is always important, key facts can often be buried in press releases and her performance earlier in the championship is important.

Showing great balance and strength she reaped the dividends of a difficult routine tariff to score 14.333 points, finishing behind Romania's Catalina Ponor and Larisa Iordache, who won gold and silver respectively.

Whelan, the reigning British all-round champion, then produced a perfectly executed floor routine to claim another third place.

Important detail to include that she is the British champion.

Iordache and Ponor again took the other medals, although their positions were reversed from the beam final.

It completed an encouraging week for the British team, with Gabrielle Jupp winning bronze in the junior floor event and 15-year-olds Rebecca

Tunney and Ruby Harrold, both making their senior debuts, reaching apparatus finals.

Whelan admitted her success was unexpected and claimed it would only boost her confidence as she seeks selection to a second Olympics.

Some of the quotes were quite bland and clichéd – 'I'm over the moon' etc. The reported speech above enables you to edit this out.

'I wanted to come out and enjoy the competition and I definitely did. I enjoy training beam and feel naturally comfortable on it and to get our first ever medal on that piece is very special,' she said.

'I've always dreamed of getting major medals and to come away with two is unbelievable.'

This is the best quote selection from what was provided in the press release. Now try condensing the material down, say, to 100 words:

Hannah Whelan claimed double bronze – including Britain's first-ever major beam medal – at the European Gymnastics Championships in Brussels.

It's still the strongest intro, summing up the story in the most concise way.

British all-around champion Whelan also finished third on the floor to complete an encouraging week for the British team.

With little words to play with, scores and other medallists can get trimmed because they are not integral to the story.

Gabrielle Jupp won bronze in the junior floor event and 15-year-olds Rebecca Tunney and Ruby Harrold, both reached senior apparatus finals.

'I enjoy training beam and feel naturally comfortable on it and to get our first-ever medal on that piece is very special,' said Whelan, who is looking to secure a second Olympic selection after her debut in Beijing.

This is the strongest quote to include if you have to make a selection.

Again the more you practise, the more you improve. Press releases are often published on official websites – look under the section titled 'Media' – so there are plenty of resources out there to use. Try changing the number of words you need – remember it's not about really clever writing. If the number of words needed is just 80, you'll need to say as much as you can in the fewest words possible. Also, set yourself harder deadlines. Can you turn around a press release like the one above into a 150-word story in just 20 minutes?

Remember the key lessons:

- Get the lead right and the rest should follow.
- Always look to lead on a name, either someone with a reputation or pedigree, such as an international or major-championship medal winner, or the person who stood out – this factor always applies to team sports.
- Be prepared for the best line to be buried in the press release – the strongest quote or most newsworthy fact, for example.
- Cut out PR speak, such as, 'I'm delighted to be working with Trident Motors as their new sports ambassador.'
- Quotes are not essential, but if they add to the article then there is no harm to include them. It obviously depends on the length of the copy you are writing.
- Sponsors are integral to sport, so it's appropriate to leave them in copy where editorially relevant, particularly if they have naming rights to a tournament; examples include the AEGON Championships, Heineken Cup and Virgin London Marathon.

7

BIG READ

FEATURE WRITING AND INTERVIEWS

The first rule to good feature writing is to forget the rules. The straitjacket that is often applied to news stories is removed and the journalist gets the chance to go more in-depth and add colour, analysis and comment. Readers don't expect to have the whole story summed up within the first few paragraphs – by reading a feature they are preparing to invest more time in your copy and the 'Five Ws' rule should not be so rigidly applied. There should be no textbook for writing features. Each feature writer applies their own personal style. If everyone constructed features in the same way, they would soon lose their appeal as the colour of a newspaper compared to the often black and white of news.

This style is honed with experience and drawn from many sources. Some feature writers are witty, some scale literary heights with their elegant prose, others force their opinions and the best deliver their desired content unobtrusively so their subject matter, rather than themselves, shines through. But the basic rules of journalism still apply. You need to grab the reader's attention and keep it, which can be much harder to do when you are dealing with longer word counts.

You need to intrigue the reader enough – persuade them that it's worth going on with your story rather than doing something else and, ideally, you need to deliver a kicker at the conclusion that will ensure your piece is retweeted, shared, passed on or just remembered. Ask most trainee journalists what they aspire to and the majority answer they want to write features. From the outside it looks the most glamorous of assignments. But feature writing is incredibly hard. Done well, copy flows beautifully and effortlessly, with interwoven story arcs, themes and subplots. The reader is carried through them on a velvet carpet of elegant words, which have been rewritten and polished then rewritten and polished again. Done badly, features can judder and jar, confuse and confound. For a subeditor, a bad feature is the worst possible thing to work on. A news story can easily be tweaked into shape or even rewritten from just stripping out and reordering the facts. However, it is so much harder to do with a feature.

Statistics aren't on the side of aspiring feature writers either. Studies have revealed that even when selecting to read a story, either online or in a newspaper, a large number of readers don't finish it. In tabloid newspapers, it's only 57 per cent. This increased to 62 per cent in broadsheets and 77 per cent online and those numbers fall as the length of the story increases. Studies also show that it takes between four and five minutes to read 1000 words and maintaining interest for this period should not be taken lightly.

Charlie Byrne, a recent graduate of an NCTJ training course at journalism school News Associates, who is now working for Sky Sports and Channel Four, says:

> How many features have you started to read and then nodded off by the third paragraph? I try to put myself in the reader's shoes and think about what I'd like to pick up and read. You have to be excited and enthusiastic about your idea or it won't translate in your writing.

So capturing the attention span of your readers, who are just one click or finger flick away from another story, is vital. Much like a good match report or news story the key to this remains your introduction and the more expansive style of feature gives you a number of options for this. A dropped intro ignores the impact or essence of the story but is written in such a way that readers are slowly drawn into the feature. By the time they are reading the key information, you hope they invested enough in the copy to go all the way to the final paragraph.

For example, this interview with Lance Armstrong before he attempted to win his seventh, and ultimately, final Tour de France title:

> Maggie Barton claims to be Lance Armstrong's biggest fan and boasts a tattoo to prove it. In her Texas souvenir shop, in a typical out-of-town mall on the outskirts of his Austin hometown, she sells cowboy boots, cowboy hats and even cowboy chaps, which are available for ages three and upwards.
>
> However, for just $20 you can buy one of her specialty Armstong t-shirts, with 'In Lance We Trust' and 'Call it the Tour de Lance and be done with it'.
>
> But the best seller comes in any colour – as long as it is yellow. On the front it proclaims: 'France 0 USA 6' while the back features Armstrong's image surrounded with the words: 'Don't Mess with Texas'.
>
> Maggie is in no doubt that 'her man' will be triumphant on the Champs Elysees in 22 days. 'It's a done deal, dahling,' she drawls.
>
> If only the same could be said of the man himself.

The feature then moves into an interview with Armstrong, over another 2000-plus words, in which he previews in great detail his hopes for the race. However, the first quarter of the piece makes no mention of these quotes, with the author hoping the headline and picture used and his approach to the intro will be enough to tease interest.

You would never start a news story with a quote but this is perfectly acceptable in feature writing. It could be a quote from the person in the feature, a poem or a play – it could set up a theme that runs through your piece from intro to outro, the sign-off line that should neatly tie everything together. It's also worth remembering that in a feature, how you end the article is as important as how you start it.

In news stories or 'on the whistle' match reports, events tend to be presented in newsworthy order, so if cutting for space, a subeditor will focus attention on the final few paragraphs. It's different with features, however, and getting the ending right is important. A standard tactic is to use the theme of the intro to tie the piece together. A good feature tempts the readers in, entertains them and leaves them satisfied with a well-executed pay-off. The first paragraph might read, 'Tiger Woods has spent the week prowling Royal Liverpool's scorched savannah with the fresh meat of his Open rivals in his predatory sights.' The final paragraph, 'But don't doubt the former champion – he has the scent of the kill in his nostrils once again.'

You would never ask a question in a news story. But you can in a feature. For example:

They came in their thousands and watched in their millions. They had just one question. Could their beloved horse defy the odds, the ravages of time and all previously proven sporting logic and win?

There are plenty of variations on these themes and it is also possible to combine them, but with a feature the intro is everything. Why would anyone read your second paragraph if you don't capture them with the first? However, every feature needs a theme, an angle or a peg on which it should be hung, such as an upcoming event, the release of a book or an anniversary of an achievement.

But a good feature adds depth – maybe takes a sideways glance at the obvious line, which could be covered elsewhere. Sportsbeat's executive editor David Parsons says:

In the build-up to the Olympics we sent a reporter to cover to launch of the British synchronised swimming team. The top line was obviously that these girls had earned their selection but the quotes were pretty fluffy – 'I'm really happy', 'it's a once-in-a-lifetime experience' etc. The reporter instead focused her feature on how long each of the girls could hold her breath, their crazy training schedule and some of the bizarre injuries they'd received. It made for a much more interesting read and told me and hopefully the reader something they didn't know about a sport that doesn't get much media coverage. So don't be predictable with features, be prepared to take a few risks – the worst that could happen is your copy is thrown back at you!

An English journalist once described his counterparts on the sports desks of Scottish newspapers as 'fans with typewriters' – claiming they had lost all sense of balance and objectivity to their writing. Go to any bar post-match and you'll see that sports journalists don't tend to hold back on their opinions, but a frequent criticism – usually made by athletes – is the journalists should be in no position to criticise when they've not played sport at the highest level. Of course, some former sportspeople graduate seamlessly to the media, realising that they are being paid for their expert opinion and should express it, without fear of upsetting those they may once have played against or alongside. John McEnroe is the world's most in-demand tennis commentator, while Michael Atherton, in both the written and spoken word, is perhaps already a more-accomplished journalist than he was England cricket captain.

Unfortunately, there are exceptions to the accepted rule with a plethora of talking heads offering anodyne opinions that do little or nothing to enhance coverage. Sportswriters will argue that just because the highlight of their sporting careers was a hat-trick when playing for their local team's under-11s, that doesn't prevent them from being part of the conversation. They see themselves as a conduit between the fan and the club or individual, and too often an athlete who moves into the media lacks objectivity.

One way sports journalists can understand a sport better is to put their reputation on the line with participatory features. Frequently, sports that want to increase their profile offer journalists the chance to 'have a go' in a bid to improve their understanding. British sportswriter Ian Stafford took this further in his acclaimed and recommended book *Playgrounds of the Gods*, in which he played squash with Jansher Khan, boxed with Roy Jones, Jr, was a sub for the Springboks versus Ireland, was 12th man for the Australian cricket team in a one-dayer against New Zealand, competed in the Kenyan 3000m steeplechase national trials and rowed with Steve Redgrave at the Henley Royal Regatta.

Ian Wooldridge, the fabled sportswriter on the *Daily Mail*, went one step further, running with bulls in Pamplona, attempting the trans-Alaska dog race, sparring with Ugandan dictator Idi Amin and riding down the fabled Cresta Run, a sheet-ice bobsleigh track in St Moritz, Switzerland. He wrote of this adventure:

> Yesterday we rode the Cresta Run. To be more accurate we bounced down it like a pinball. After careful thought I declare it to be the greatest thrill that life has to offer ... I am not proud at all to confess I was so enduringly terrified that I doubt I shall ever do it again.

In addition to having a go, participatory features can include looking behind the scenes at a sporting event, perhaps riding in a team car on a cycle race, observing a sailing regatta from race control or watching a motorsport event from inside a team garage on the pit lane.

Furniture pieces

Many newspapers and websites have regular features that aim to break up content. These are sometimes referred to as furniture pieces because they appear frequently and always follow the same theme. For example, it could be a picture of a famous sporting moment – the anniversary of which is being celebrated – with reference back to what was written 5, 10, 20 years ago and perhaps bringing the story up to date by reporting what those involved are now doing. Fans might frequently say, 'Do you remember X?' or 'I wonder what happened to Y?', journalists Andy Pringle and Neil Fissler wrote a book titled *Where Are They Now?* that was derived from a regular newspaper feature of the same name. Using their contacts, connections and research skills, they were able to take a number of teams and report what players were now doing who had slipped from public view. Many were just living normal lives, but others became millionaire businessmen, vicars and comedians. One even became the finance minister of Iceland.

Other furniture pieces include items like the 60-second interview, a series of quick-fire questions such as 'What keeps you awake at night?' or 'Who would be your three ideal dinner party guests?' There are other variations on this theme such as 'My first, my last', which asks questions like 'When was the last time you got drunk?' or 'What was your first car?' The answers to these questions are unlikely to be strong enough to lead a feature or be worthy of a news headline but they do give fans the chance to learn something new about athletes. For example, did you know that David Beckham's first car was a Ford Escort?

Jim White is an award-winning feature writer at the *Daily Telegraph*, a regular contributor to BBC Radio Five Live and the author of *You'll Win Nothing with Kids*, a much-praised book which chronicles his time as manager of his son's football team. He gives these tips for budding feature writers:

- Feature ideas are often a product of collaboration and scanning forthcoming events.
- When you are starting out, blogs are useful for honing skills, learning how to write and demonstrating aptitude, although not so useful for gaining prominence.
- On a scale of 1 to 10, where 10 is tremendously important, then contacts are 11.
- Timing has changed with the written press but Twitter and the internet are useful for teasing stories and using as a trailer for printed material.
- It's a tough industry but, in many ways, I think the process of trying to find a job will prove whether you have the aptitude for it.
- My best advice is the relentless use of contacts, don't take no for an answer, don't be put off by disappointment or rudeness and keep going when others will give up.
- Do all that in pursuit of a job and you'll do the job well.

A feature writer needs to maintain a constant stream of ideas, because many of the items they might put up for publication will not be commissioned. A good knowledge of sporting history is important. When Jessica Ennis went for heptathlon gold at the London 2012 Olympics, fellow British athlete Mary Peters, who won the equivalent event 40 years earlier, became an in-demand interviewee.

Most features are conceived, written and published in a relatively short timeframe – although most sports desks have a stock of timeless articles that can be used at short notice if something happens, weather decimates the sporting programme or something falls through. However, long lead features can involve journalists, usually those working on magazines, going into deep background, perhaps spending a period of time researching their subject matter. For example, a journalist could be given privileged access to a club, athlete or major-event organising committee over a period of weeks and months. Publication of the story will then be timed for maximum impact.

Journalists continually moan about their access to athletes, how it is controlled by PR handlers and how media training has taught sportspeople to speak and yet say nothing that is remotely noteworthy. Tennis players are particularly good at this, obliged to attend media commitments by tournament organizers. It's possible to sit through a 10-minute Roger Federer or Rafael Nadal press conference and realise you've not got a single newsworthy quote. But while access has certainly contracted for journalists, the public's access to athletes has increased. Athletes are more informed and knowledgeable about their achievements than ever before, with many taking the roll of self-publishers with their own websites and Twitter accounts.

Contacts are vital when it comes to setting up interviews. Usually, they will be facilitated by media departments or agents and, increasingly, there will be a contra-arrangement whereby in return for access, the journalist would agree to mention an upcoming event, sponsorship, endorsement or publication of a book.

You will now often see on many interviews in sports pages an end credit or boilerplate, for example:

> Wayne Rooney was speaking on behalf of Betfair – the home of football rivalry where fans bet against each other. For the latest footy news, entertainment and to see exclusive, behind-the-scenes content visit www.betfairfootball.com

Journalists increasingly see this commercialisation of their content as a necessary evil and just because an interview has been facilitated in this way doesn't mean the reporter should cede any control or copy approval. Your only responsibility is to make sure you treat the interviewee fairly and report their comments accurately. You should also never allow anyone to see your copy before it's published – you will get asked and the best way to dodge around this issue is to refer the person asking, normally the PR manager or the person you are interviewing, to your editor.

Sport survives on sponsorship and sponsors need to leverage the huge investments they are making. They commission media monitoring to see the reach of their sponsorship and evaluate their return on investment based on the Advertising Value Equivalent (AVE). After agreeing to back a club, team or individual, a major sponsor is usually permitted a certain number of days access for media opportunities. Depending on the exclusivity of the access being offered, journalists and their editors might also need to agree to run a branded photograph or a picture of the video game or book that the sports star is promoting. Clubs usually put up players for interview ahead of major matches, selecting them depending on the topicality of the game, recent form or whether they are newsworthy. They usually try to share these duties around the club, so different players get a chance for media exposure. The clubs control this process and, because the media departments of most major clubs are run by former journalists, they know the sort of questions likely to be asked. So if a player is going back to his old club, where he had spectacularly fallen out with the manager or coach, don't expect his new employer to allow them to speak in advance of the match because the club know the obvious angle and direction the media will take that story.

One-on-one interviews

Interviews in advance of major events are pretty tightly controlled. They may take the form of a coach or player giving several interviews to different media groups, one-on-ones with television and radio and a round table with written press. If written press want to keep some degree of exclusivity over their material, they may do their interviews separately for agencies and internet sites, who publish content immediately. In the UK, journalists from Sunday newspapers might also do their interviews separately. They will look for a 'Sunday line' that will differentiate their copy from their colleagues on daily newspaper titles.

Sometimes interviews are arranged under embargo, with the journalists agreeing not to publish until a certain hour or day. When setting up the interview, you will be asked where the interview will appear and what subject matter it will cover – but you don't have to reveal every question you will ask, just a broad outline. It is also worth establishing how long you will have to conduct the interview because that will directly influence your strategy for questioning. Some sports stars are notoriously monosyllabic, so you need time to ease them into a conversation and hopefully get them feeling more at ease with you.

In reality no interview – except for a long profile piece – needs to take more than 30 minutes, indeed 10 to 15 minutes of good questioning can elicit more than enough material for a good length piece. It's always worth remembering that most athletes tolerate media work. They see it as a distraction, but only a few really enjoy it. Ideally, you would avoid doing interviews too close or too soon after competition because their focus is inevitably elsewhere, although sometimes you just have to work with the slot you are given.

If journalists had a choice, then all interviews would be done face to face. Eye contact, so important to building a rapport, is impossible when interviewing over the telephone. However, sometimes it may not be possible for reasons of timing, budget or geography to interview in person. You could use Skype or a similar programme – most athletes are pretty savvy about these due to the amount of time they spend travelling and keeping in touch with friends and family from long distances.

Occasionally, you will be told to submit a list of questions and supplied with written answers, but good pieces rarely come from this approach (interviews should flow like a natural conversation), although again sometimes you don't have a choice. While you will have an idea of the questions you want to ask, you can follow up or seek clarification if something is unclear. In reality, you also know that it is unlikely the athletes have written the answers themselves, more probably they've been provided by agents or their PR teams.

Some publications like to run Q&A-style interview features, which is basically an ordered list of the questions and the answers they solicited. Some athletes like these because they're the best way to ensure their answers are not selectively edited or spun to fit in with a certain predetermined news agenda. Journalists would prefer to stamp their own mark on interview features but if presented in this form the pressure is on to ask interesting questions that generate good answers.

Whatever style of feature you are producing you want to avoid asking closed questions that lead to one word responses. Which of these questions is likely to give a better answer:

- Can you tell me what you enjoyed about that victory?
- You must have enjoyed that victory?
- Were you disappointed with the sending off?
- What was your opinion of the sending off?

There is a difference in interviewing technique depending on when you are doing it. After competition, the agenda is obviously set by what has just happened on the field of play. As a radio or television journalist, your question is part of the process but a print journalist just needs to ask the question that will generate the best answer. Broadcast interviews can be a performance, they have to be entertaining, but print interviews are all about the content. The question you ask is irrelevant, it's the answer that matters.

After a match or competition a straightforward, 'What are your thoughts on that performance?' is usually the best way to start off a conversation. But set the tone – if the interview is a one-on-one and the athlete is not known to you introduce yourself and the publication that you work for. Congratulate the athlete if they have done well and commiserate if not. Tom Reynolds, who graduated from journalism school four years ago and now works as a reporter at British press agency Sportsbeat, says:

Ninety per cent of what is said after a match or competition is pretty bland. However, sometimes the emotion of the moment changes that.

I was covering one sport when an athlete stepped off the track after a particularly disappointing performance and then lambasted her coach.

It still wasn't my lead story, I was just blobbing the result and a couple of quotes paragraphs on the end of my piece. I told the press officer what I had and offered to give the athlete 10 minutes to calm down and think about her quotes – she wasn't a big name and the piece would have been buried but it would have still had lasting ramifications for her relationship with the team and coach.

Sure enough after the athlete had calmed down, she came back out, thanked me and gave me different, although less fiery quotes. More importantly for me I had proven to the team that I was someone who could be trusted and I got much better stories and opportunities afforded to me in the long run.

For interviews set up as features, profiles or match previews, you will take a different approach. Again research is key. Find out as much about the subject as you can. If the person is not well known, they will appreciate the effort you've made and you'll be rewarded with better quotes. Nothing smacks of lazy journalism more than a reporter who uses interview time to check background information that they easily could have gained by doing some simple researching. You should also know you rivals and check the internet for recent interviews to make sure you don't get the same set of quotes and end up with virtually the same story that has already been published elsewhere.

You might have several options on how to angle your story. Writing out a list of questions might be useful but be prepared to adapt this depending on the answers. One of the most important skills in interviewing is listening. You will then be able to respond better to the answers you are given and probe further with follow-up questions if you think they are required. Imagine this exchange:

Q. Can you tell me how your winter training has been going?
A. It's been awful to be honest, I had an ankle ligament problem, then I was struck down by glandular fever. There were days I thought there was no point in continuing, I seriously considered jacking it all in.
Q. What are you expectations for this summer?

Clearly the answer above needs to be expanded. This could well be the whole thrust of the story but the interviewer has stuck too rigidly to the script. If you don't understand something, don't be afraid to seek clarification, particularly if it's a technical detail perhaps in a minority sport. If you've been told something contentious but you are still confused about where the interviewee is coming from, ask the question again.

Tom Barclay graduated from his NCTJ qualification at News Associates three years ago and now works for the sports desk at the *Sun*, Britain's biggest-selling newspaper. He says:

> It depends on whom you are interviewing but with more preparation and a game plan going into an interview, you have a better chance of getting the individual revealing something fresh and entertaining. I've only been doing this a few years, so I'm far from a master at it but I know that preparation is the difference between a good interview and dull one full of fluff.
>
> One of the techniques I'm learning very quickly is that if you're gunning for a particular angle on something, don't be afraid to ask the question more than once. For instance, if you ask them your key question and they give you a unsatisfactory answer, push them on it. And then push them again if they still don't bite. Of course, you need to know when to quit but sometimes the best quotes come from the second or third time of asking.
>
> Planning the order of your questions can be crucial. It depends on how long you have with the interviewee but generally you want to warm them up with a few questions before going in with the key question. It sounds stupid but do your best to really listen to what they are saying. That might sound obvious but when you are interviewing someone you are too often thinking about the next question. You need to be able to react if they say something that you were not expecting.

The most important thing in an interview is the answers – the journalist should try not to impose on the conversation – but you have to get the balance right between the interviewer and the interviewee. Those who are experienced in dealing with the media, in particularly politicians and sports administrators, are adept at not answering the question and, occasionally, talking down the clock of an interview, saying nothing of real note or only giving bland comments that you could easily read in a press release. You can't let the balance of an interview tip too much in their favour. David Parsons, the executive editor at the press agency Sportsbeat remembers:

> I recall interviewing a former sports minister over the phone quite early in my career. I asked one question and he spoke non-stop, despite my attempts, probably quite half-hearted, to interject. He finally finished

and said, 'I think I've given you enough for a story there' and put the phone down.

There are tips for interrupting if the answer you are being given is becoming incredibly long-winded or starting to stray widely off topic. No one wants to be misquoted so you could – if all else fails – interject and say, 'Excuse me, I want to make sure I get this right but could you just explain ...' This approach often allows you the chance to reset the conversation back in your favour. Obviously if you have a particularly contentious question, one that you think might elicit a negative reaction don't ask it at the top of the interview.

If a television or radio interviewer manages to irritate someone so much that they storm off, the interviewer would probably consider that a bit of a result. It makes for good broadcasting to see people rattled, the clips goes viral on YouTube – remember Kevin Keegan's rant about Alex Ferguson during the 1996 Premier League season? The stock of the interviewer probably only rises too. If that happens to a print journalist, then you're just left with a lot of words to fill. Worse still, if you are sharing your interview with colleagues in a round-table set-up or at a press conference, you might have to contend with their ire too. However, difficult questions are part of the job and, most of the time, the person you are interviewing is expecting them.

Awkward questions

There are times when you might have to broach hard subjects, such as a bereavement. While you always worry about how to phrase these questions and worry about intrusion, you often find people find discussing such issues cathartic. Also, you will occasionally be told certain subjects are off limits. Sometimes, it's impossible not to ignore if the topic is really in the news. It will be up to the journalist to negotiate this with whoever is handling the PR, but remember you have to keep in mind what the fans would want to read.

If a team has just lost to a late controversial penalty and the PR comes in before the manager and says, 'Don't ask him about the spot kick please', it would make a bit of a mockery of the interview. Journalists are in a privileged position that fans would love to be in – they need to ask the questions they want answering. There are ways around this of course, such as, 'Were you happy with the referee's performance today?' And if you leave your question until last and it's not answered, it's a bit of a free hit, although you risk potentially isolating yourself – and you should always bear in mind how important access is.

Another tip you need to prepare for when interviewing is the throwback question, when the interviewee turns the tables on you. You want to avoid pointed questions where possible, they can needlessly irritate, but sometimes people can easily take offence. If you are going to ask a difficult question, have facts to back it up, know your brief or you will be exposed and run the risk of being embarrassed. For example:

Q. Are you disappointed with your defending in recent weeks?
A. Why should I be?

It's a good trick taught in media training courses. Deflect the question or refuse to accept the premise of the question. It puts the interviewer on the back foot and tips the balance of the conversation against you. So be prepared to answer back, politely, and try to move on, for example:

Well you had one of the meanest defences at the start of the season but in contrast you've let nine goals in the last three games. Do you think it's a temporary problem?

Shorthand: a journalist's best friend

The most important thing with an interview is to get down what you are told accurately. The overwhelming majority of journalists use Dictaphones or recording devices. Most of these are now digital. Many journalists even use their mobile phone or a plug-in adaptor on their digital audio player, which saves the worry that you will suddenly run out of tape. Files can then be downloaded and saved on to your laptop and it is advisable to keep evidence of interviews for up to six months, even after you've transcribed them, in case any issues are raised with your published story. The problem with recording interviews is they take a long time to transcribe – to get down a verbatim transcript of a 20-minute interview can take nearly an hour. Therefore, many reporters rely on their shorthand, an abbreviated writing method that increases speed or brevity of writing.

There are several versions of shorthand, with most journalists now trained in Teeline to an industry standard 100 words per minute. When on a deadline, especially after a match or event, this form of note-taking is much quicker than listening back to a conversation, pausing, rewinding, pausing and rewinding your recording device. If you have more time with your feature, then a Dictaphone and no note-taking, allowing you to fully concentrate on your subject matter, probably works better. However, you will find most journalists combine the two methods, depending on the circumstance. Dennis Campbell, a former sports reporter, now covering health stories, on the *Observer*, says:

> If a manager walks into a press room at 10 p.m. after a Champions League semi-final and talks for 10 minutes and the reporter has until 10.30 p.m. to file 400 of their choicest words – a typical scenario – then not having shorthand will leave him unable to provide the necessary copy by deadline.

A tape recorder gets it exactly, but is laborious to transcribe. And one's fellow reporters who do have shorthand will be too busy writing furiously to share it with you, as they'll be up against their deadline too. So what will the journalist without shorthand do then? Campbell can't stress the importance of shorthand enough:

> It seems to me that in the integrated media age more reporters are going to have to file more copy more often for more outlets, at least from big events – sports tournaments, court cases, big running stories etc. – as they'll be filing for their paper's website, as well as the paper product. Time will be even more precious than it is now. So shorthand will be even more important.

If you get the chance to decide on a location for the interview, always try to do it where the interviewee will be at their most relaxed. The more confident and at ease they are the better the quality of material you will gain. In advance of the London 2012 Olympics, media sessions were held for the announcement of every team and a preparation camp, with stipulated access for every athlete, was staged.

However, these sorts of surroundings rarely produce really good in-depth copy as the athletes move down a production line of representatives from TV, radio and the written press. Better still, make the effort to meet athletes on their home patch, such as a racehorse trainer at his stables, a golfer for a drink in the bar of his local club, or perhaps even in the sportsperson's home. Sometimes, where the interview is staged is a main hook for the feature, such as an athlete returning to a stadium where they have had success or visiting a former school and club. And when you get there, keep your eyes peeled for anything that could add colour to your story or generate an additional angle of questioning.

It was only when an observant interviewer, talking to Manchester United manager Alex Ferguson, saw his bookshelf crowded with history books about the American Civil War and John F. Kennedy that is became known the Manchester United manager was a US history buff. Sometimes, when time allows, it can be useful to allow interviewees to go off topic and talk about something that really interests them. You might even generate a nice quote or line from it.

However, it is always easier interviewing people who are largely unknown to a wider audience. It's much harder getting those who are regularly on television, radio or in newspapers to say something totally new. Their career, their personal life, their previous successes and failures, likes and dislikes have already been widely reported and are just a Google search away. But it is said there isn't a single person in the world that you can't get to talk about themselves. And a skilled interviewer knows that when people talk, and they feel at ease, even when they've been drilled in media training, they often reveal more than they really want to.

A good interviewer lets them talk, interjects only to guide the conversation and ease and tease out any revelations that may be forthcoming. When it comes to writing up your interview or profile piece, the rigid rules of news writing and the flexibility of feature writing apply. If it is a post-event reaction story you will probably go for quite a newsy line, which ideally throws itself forward. For example, 'Rory McIlroy insists he has learned the lessons from his back-nine horror show at Augusta and has vowed to put it in at the US Open', or 'Mo Farah believes he's only going to get quicker after storming to a new personal best in his final race before the Olympics'.

Jonathan Northcroft, the football correspondent of the *Sunday Times*, urges journalists to follow three golden rules of interviewing: prepare, make it a conversation not an interrogation and take time to digest all your material as opposed to rushing to decide the line of a story.

My interview preparation has changed over the years – though the principle that you should prepare as thoroughly as possible has endured.

I start with an idea of why it might be interesting to speak to that person, but try to be open-minded about exactly what lines of questioning I'll employ before I've done some reading. This will involve a quick web search to establish context and 'back story' (Wikipedia, Google, the club website, the player's personal website) and then a more detailed statistical look at the person (Soccerbase, zonalmarking, WhoScored.com and the Premier League/EA sports stats sites are good).

What I'm trying to do here is find out stats/facts that point to something perhaps unnoticed about that person (e.g. the defender who turns out to have a fantastic passing/scoring record etc.). I might then look at the stats from a couple of key games that a player has been involved in (if I were interviewing Drogba, I'd want to look at his stats in the Champions League final for example).

The next stage of prep would be to read previous newspaper interviews that player has done. Some journos use ClipShare, some use their newspaper's own libraries. I prefer to use the Dow Jones 'Factiva' site. What I'm looking for here is twofold: little nuggets of info/personal detail that could be expanded on in a piece; but also what should I avoid repeating, that the player has said in other interviews? There's nothing worse than feeling you've come up with a good story about someone only to realize they covered the same subject/story in the *Sunday Telegraph* six months previously!

That's the reading stage – the next thing to do is try and speak to people who might know the player. If I know the player's manager, and have his number or will be seeing him at a briefing, I'll ask about the player. I might call the player's agent (they are often a good source of stories, because it's in their interest to ensure their client comes out of the interview looking interesting!). It might involve calling another player. It might even involve calling a fellow journalist, who you know is acquainted with the player. This is especially useful when it comes to foreign players – before interviewing van Persie once, I called a good mate in the Dutch press and it turned out he'd known Robin since he was 9, and had loads of stories about him.

Once I've gathered all this info, I start thinking about questions and here's where my prep has changed over the years. Early on I think I made the mistake of trying to cover absolutely every interesting thing I'd discovered in my research in the interview. It meant I'd have a huge list of questions across different subjects and it was difficult to ask them all in the time allotted and to make the interview flow.

The best interviews flow like natural conversations – you have to be ready to go with the subject if they start getting passionate about something, or follow up an unexpected statement or interesting nugget of info they divulge.

Longer interview features or profiles have less rules applied, depending on the style of the publication you are writing for, so you might have the opportunity to be more expansive and use some of the different methods described earlier in this chapter. You don't have to get to the killer quote straight away, just aim to slowly draw the readers in, maintain their attention and then hit them with your best material. For example:

He's plotting a course to become arguably the most decorated British sailor since Nelson but for a man who spends so much time on water, Ben Ainslie is admirably grounded.

Ainslie was just 19 – even more prodigious than the dashing young midshipman Horatio – when he won silver in Atlanta. Three Olympic titles have followed to mean Ainslie now has more gold medals on his chest than an Admiral of the Fleet and is considered one of Britain's home medal bankers for this summer's Olympics.

After you've concluded your interview, it is sensible to transcribe your notes as quickly as possible. However, immediately after the interview has ended, you will probably have a pretty good idea of the best material and an intro or theme for your story will already be taking shape. But remember this is an interview and the reader wants to read about the subject matter, not the journalist. From your transcript, highlight your strongest material, which will probably be used as direct quotations in your article. Sometimes, the quotes are so powerful that the article needs the lightest touch from the journalist. The job is then to present the material in the way that has the most impact – a strong intro, a couple of paragraphs for context and then let the quotes speak for themselves.

Back in 1995, Italian cyclist and Olympic gold medallist Fabio Casartelli died at the Tour de France. Years later, I interviewed his father about his recollections of that tragic day. His story and quotes were incredibly moving and after I'd transcribed them I realised that I was struggling to decide what to omit. I didn't want to use reported speech, when a father is talking about his adored son who has passed away. I believed the reader should not get my interpretation of his comments. I kept my piece simple, three paragraphs to open up for context and then let the quotes run, breaking in occasionally with a couple more paragraphs of background information so the quotes could be contextualised. I didn't feel the need to think of a clever intro, I just wanted to present the material in the best way possible.

But in the majority of cases, the interviewer will mix direct quotations with reported speech, which helps vary the pace of the copy – and as ever it's a case of striking the right balance. Take the quotes below, just under 200 words transcribed from an interview with the aforementioned Olympian Ben Ainslie:

There is always a bit of fear when you step back into a class after a spell out. You worry that things might have moved on while you have been away or that you are so far off the pace that to catch up with the rest of the guys is an impossibility. But I feel good at the moment.

It was always going to take a while to get back to my peak fitness. I'm getting there and I'm pretty confident that by the summer, with all the hard work, I should be where I need to be.

I spent two months in Australia over the new year and sailing in really big breezes really helped with my fitness.

It is amazing how the body adapts and the only way you can get anywhere near getting back to full sailing fitness is by getting out there and putting yourself through all things your body is not familiar with doing anymore.

It takes time to get your body used to all the strains you get sailing a Finn again, but I'm definitely feeling less aches and pains now.

By mixing direct quotes with reported speech the journalist is able to condense this down to just over 130 words:

Ainslie claims to be feeling good after two months training in Australia but admits he experienced some trepidation about returning to the class after a spell out.

'It was always going to take a while to get back to my peak fitness,' he said.

'I'm getting there and I'm pretty confident that by the summer, with all the hard work, I should be where I need to be.

'It is amazing how the body adapts and the only way you can get anywhere near getting back to full sailing fitness is by getting out there and putting yourself through all things your body is not familiar with doing anymore.

'It takes time to get your body used to all the strains you get sailing a Finn again but I'm definitely feeling less aches and pains now.'

Tidying up speech

Unfortunately, people don't tend to talk in neatly formed sentences, they um and they ah and they stop sentences in mid-flow and go off at tangents. Journalists should always quote accurately but there is no problem with tidying up grammar or editing down rambling speech, providing the thrust of the quote is not being changed. And, of course, if someone makes a factual inaccuracy in their quote, perhaps referring to someone as the defending champion when they have already been deposed, you can correct it.

Here is the verbatim transcript, provided by ASAP Sports, of what Andy Murray said after losing in the 2011 Wimbledon semi-final to Rafael Nadal:

Q: You're saying you're going to take a few days, you generally can recover from something like this quite quickly. Can you explain what you'll do over the next coming days and what you can learn from today?

MURRAY: Work harder than I ever did before. Try and improve my game and get stronger. Be more professional. Yeah, try and learn from what happened today. Yeah, think about the things that I need to improve.

Yeah, that's all you can do. You've just got to work harder than you have done in the past to get better. It's a very tough era I think in tennis. Tennis right at the top of the game is exceptional. So not only to get level with those guys, but to push past them, you need to work harder than them. That's what I need to try to do.

This is how it was reported the following day, some words were inserted to make the structure make sense and sentences were joined up to improve the flow but the context remains the same.

'I need to work harder than I ever did before,' said Murray. 'I have to try and improve my game, get stronger and be more professional. I need to learn from what happened and think about the things that I need to improve.

'That's all you can do. You've just got to work harder than you have done in the past to get better. It's a very tough era and the tennis right at the top of the game is exceptional.'

Fig 7.1 Media wait in the mixed zone at Wimbledon following Andy Murray's Olympic men's singles tennis gold medal

8

BIG OPINIONS

COLOUR WRITING AND COLUMNS

With only a few notable exceptions, most great reporters are not great writers and most great writers are not great reporters but any publication needs both in equal measure. Nowhere does this apply more than the sports pages. Sometimes, you want the story, sometimes you want the story behind the story and sometimes you don't want the story at all – you just want to be entertained.

Sports journalists have often been subject to jibes about their profession from colleagues at the newspaper. The 'back of the book' – as it is known – was derided as a toyshop and sportswriters were dubbed 'groin strains'. While those in news section of the paper worried about matters of state and foreign affairs, their colleagues in sport were more concerned about a broken metatarsal and troublesome Achilles tendon.

But nothing drives newspaper sales like sport. It remains the richest source of advertising revenue, online and offline. Compare the traffic surge a website would experience if England won the World Cup to a Prime Minister resigning. It's also true that the best writing in any newspaper can frequently be found on the sports pages. When the *Mail on Sunday* was looking for someone to write an elegant and emotive account of the funeral service of Diana, Princess of Wales, in 1997, the newspaper turned to its chief sports-writer Patrick Collins to describe the historic occasion. A good writer should be able to give you 1000 words on the inside of a ping-pong ball and still make it interesting.

Adding colour

A colour piece usually sits alongside a match report or news story in a bid to add depth to coverage and give the fan another perspective. Much like profile interviews and features, there are no rules for its construction but good colour writing will turn prose into poetry, show courage of convictions and not be afraid to take a risk and, above all, it will entertain. Done well, nothing looks easier than colour writing. In reality, it's one of the hardest things to do. Some pieces are okay, most are good but very few are brilliant. It's a sobering thought for any aspiring journalist.

I remember early in my career attending a rugby union international at Twickenham and sitting just a desk behind the late, great Ian Wooldridge, whose writing for the *Daily Mail* I had adored since being a youngster. It was an awful match, so bad I don't even recall whom England were playing, and my job was to provide an 'on the whistle' match report and some player ratings. But I was intrigued to watch Wooldridge at work from such close quarters for the first time. Every now and then he would tick his pad – the ticks seemed to bare no relation to the game – and he was even doing it during half time. The match concluded and little noteworthy had occurred. Two days later, I picked up the *Daily Mail* intrigued to see what the master wordsmith had crafted for his piece, given the ingredients he had to work with were so entirely unpromising. I then realised that he'd too been so bored by the encounter that he'd been counting the aircraft that had flown above the stadium. It was a brilliant line in his piece, executed with precision, and underlined what good colour writing is all about. Despite the 80,000 people in the stadium that day and millions watching on television, he still saw something no one else did and found a way to weave it into his copy and make it relevant.

In contrast to colour writing, match reports are easy. The events are unfolding in front of you. It's just a question of prioritising the best bits, weaving everything together, sprinkling through some reasoned opinion and research and hoping you hit your deadline – and also praying that nothing too decisive happens in the last few minutes.

Interviewing is all about the quotes – it's about the preparation and the questioning. But if you are writing colour at a major international event, it can be a daunting prospect. You might arrive with some ideas that you want to develop, but really you are just looking at a blank screen and hoping to be hit by a freight train of inspiration. There is no science, no formula for success – good colour writing is just good writing and good writing is incredibly difficult to produce, especially under the nagging pressure of a deadline.

The perfect colour piece will put events into a wider context, provide a commentary of accurate and well-informed insights and deliver blow after knockout blow of spot-on well-turned phrases. If you can thread through some humour and wit, and elicit a smile or even a laugh from your reader then all the better. Hugh McIlvanney, whose writing continues to grace the pages of the *Sunday Times*, remains much admired and imitated, and his soaring prose is still without parallel. On underachieving boxer Joe Bugner he wrote, 'He has the physique of a Greek statue but fewer moves.' He turned his sharpened quill on surly striker Carlos Tevez with the withering put down, 'Whatever it costs Manchester City to get rid of him is a tolerable outlay on disinfectant.' His description of England World Cup-winning captain Bobby Moore was, 'He could play tag with a fox and never get caught,' and of George Best he wrote, 'He has feet as sensitive as a pickpocket's hands.' It is beautifully elegant writing inspired by the broad range of emotions that sport generates.

However, colour writing cannot be learned it has to be practised and honed and you need to consume a large diet of what your more experienced colleagues are producing in the hope their skills will, by some process of osmosis, start to sink in. To paraphrase T.S. Eliot, good writers borrow and really great writers steal outright, so consume the labours of theatre reviewers and parliamentary sketch writers. They are doing much the same job as the sports colour writer, just with different subject matter. Producing a truly quality piece of colour reporting at the first attempt is like going around a golf course in scratch just minutes after you've bought your first set of clubs.

Writers like McIlvanney and Ian Wooldridge spent years perfecting their craft. Both started in local newspapers. McIlvanney at the *Kilmarnock Standard* and Wooldridge in his native Hampshire on the *New Milton Advertiser*. They learned the basics first and then continued to apply them even when they were given more creative licence with their copy. So if you are asked to produce a colour piece, don't worry about setting the bar too high, because you won't clear it.

It can be liberating not to have confines to your work but it can also be daunting. The rules that govern the construction of match reporting are actually helpful for those starting out in their careers. Colour writing lets them loose on a blank canvas and it can be a messy business. Colour reports need to add to the conversation – they should not just repeat the information contained within a match report or quotes pieces. So if you are working with colleagues from your outlet at an event, make sure you discuss what each other is doing.

Much like the anecdote about Ian Wooldridge counting aeroplanes, be observant. What's the mood in the crowd? Is the local funeral director the ideal match-day sponsor for a team fighting relegation? Don't be afraid to express a reasoned opinion but don't get caught up in the emotion of the moment and go over the top. You might think you've just seen a tennis match that redefined the word 'epic' but take a step back and reflect before making a judgement that once in print or online cannot be retracted. Was that strike really a contender for goal of the season or just a good goal?

Some colour reports take a theme and develop it from first to last paragraph. Take for example this rugby report. Wales had beaten England 27–18 in a Six Nations match at the Millennium Stadium. The match report lead off on the performance of Welsh fly half James Hook, who had contributed all but four of his side's points in a stand-out display. The quotes piece that ran alongside it focused on the comments of Welsh captain Gareth Thomas and the immediate thoughts of England coach Brian Ashton.

The colour piece needed to offer something else and with the World Cup just a few months away, the journalist decided to contrast the England team that had just lost with the England team that had won the title a few years earlier. He selected a theme for his copy – the television sitcom *Dad's Army* – and delivered an intro and outro, or sign-off, that pulled the piece together.

> Forget 'Bread of Heaven', Wales were last night just in heaven as they crushed their most bitter rivals in Cardiff.
>
> It's a little less than four years since England lifted the Webb Ellis Trophy with a team dubbed 'Dad's Army'.
>
> But how Brian Ashton would like Captain Mainwaring, Sergeant Wilson and Corporal Jones on his parade ground now. Instead he has been left with a squad of promising but youthful Private Pikes.
>
> And his injury-ravaged side, especially a certain fly half from Newcastle, could certainly find a role for medical orderly Godfrey and his trusty first-aid kit.
>
> Ashton might urge England fans to 'don't panic' but on the evidence of this display, any already fast-fading hopes of defending their title are already, in the immortal words of Private Frazer, 'doomed'.
>
> Retain the World Cup? Who do you think you are kiddin' Mr Ashton?

As it happened, England went on to reach the final of the World Cup later that year, losing to South Africa. So be careful with opinions. They will now be forever preserved online to haunt you. Be prepared to temper them and be prepared for those that you write about to call you on them if they don't agree. If you have an idea of a theme, be prepared for a quick rethink if what you witness requires another focus.

Just imagine you were covering Manchester City against Queens Park Rangers on the last day of the 2011–2012 Premier League season. Heading into injury time, Manchester City's hopes of winning the title were over as they were behind 2–1. You may have been preparing a post-mortem on their manager Roberto Mancini or digging into the sums to work out just how much money the club's owner had spent only to fall short of their target. But within a few seconds, Manchester City had scored twice, in the most dramatic conclusion ever to a Premier League season, and were champions. The job here for the colour writer is to contribute something that adds to the conversation in the knowledge that everyone knows the result. Millions watched on television or listened on the radio.

The *Daily Mail*'s Martin Samuel used a play on words of Kenneth Wolstenholme's famous commentary when England won the 1966 World Cup to add colour to a piece:

> There were people on the pitch and it was all over.
>
> The 44 years, over. The punchlines, over. The mockery, over. Laughing on the outside, crying on the inside, that horrid little ticker at Old Trafford, those long Monday mornings at work having to pretend you didn't really care. Over, over, over.
>
> Gone, all gone. Gone in a moment of unparalleled drama and ecstasy. Gone when all seemed lost. Gone on a day when, for 45 minutes that must have felt like hot-needle torture, it looked as if the capacity for chaos that has almost become a club trademark through five decades had returned to torment them once more.

Depending on your deadline, you might be working on two pieces at the same time, although those writing colour thankfully normally don't have to file 'on the whistle', giving them a chance to be a little more considered. But remember the emotion of covering an event. The noise, the pressure, the onrushing deadline, can play tricks. I remember writing a pretty shoddy piece about Paula Radcliffe after she pulled out of the 10,000m at the 2004 Olympics, just a few days after she did something very similar in the marathon. I started to think it was over the top as I reread my copy on the bus back to the hotel – a good tip is never go over a story after it's too late to change it – and immediately began to regret my tone. When I saw how others had handled the same story the following day, I realised how out of step I'd been and it was a salutary lesson. Take a breath, if time allows. Was that goal really sensational? Was that honestly the greatest tennis rally of all time? How incendiary were those quotes?

There is absolutely nothing wrong with having opinions that aren't widely held – although it can be a lonely place – but never be controversial for the sake of it or use hyperbole, something that afflicts so much sports journalism, unless you believe it is absolutely deserved and adds the required impact to your copy.

At its very best, sports writing can scale literary heights – inspired by amazing athletic feats and stunning comebacks – but sports journalists still have a tendency to be known for their clichés. Do people really 'turn on a sixpence'? Is it actually possible to give '110 per cent'? What does 'we need to play our game' mean? Who else's were you going to play? The most basic spellchecker will tell you that 'there's no I in team' and swimmers who vow to 'leave everything in the pool' hopefully have remembered a towel to protect their modesty.

Be original. How many times down the years do you think that a team with the nickname 'Tigers' have 'roared to victory'? How many reporters, up against a deadline and running low on creativity, have described rugby union side Wasps as being 'stung by a late try'? Occasionally, though, you can use 'cliché speak' to your benefit; it could even inspire another angle for colour writing. For example:

> For a moment it appeared the track cycling test event couldn't have gone any worse for London 2012 organisers. Having invested £105 million in what is universally being hailed as the world's best velodrome, it took just 6000 excitable fans to – in the words of the official stadium announcer – 'blow the roof clean off'. And that was just the qualifying for the women's team pursuit at a World Cup meeting.
>
> Imagine what could happen in a final … at the Olympics? You just hope that Seb Coe and his crew ordered strengthened foundations and bribed health and safety with a pair of tickets to the 100m final or an 'access all areas' accreditation for the beach volleyball.
>
> Then, as Britain scampered to two golds and two world records on the track's opening finals night, the man with the microphone reported, breathlessly, that people were 'literally bursting with pride'. Danny Boyle was fuming. People 'bursting with pride' was going to be a spectacular show-stopper for his opening ceremony.
>
> A quick call to St John Ambulance thankfully revealed no fatalities, although someone had reportedly choked on a peanut, underlining the dangers of enjoying bar snacks of any kind while watching Victoria Pendleton. But even worse news followed on Saturday morning. *The Times*, our very own paper of record, splashed a headline on their front page that British cyclists had 'set the velodrome alight.' How's that for gratitude? You lavish them with lottery funding and build them a

gleaming new facility with the fastest track in the world and they repay you by becoming a bunch of unruly pyromaniacs.

Avoid puns

Puns fall into the same category as clichés and should be avoided. Tim Henman's valiant march to the semi-finals at Wimbledon was frequently described as 'Henmania', although it finally proved a summer affliction more irritating than hay fever. Jeremy Lin's breakthrough with the NY Nicks was variously described as 'Linsanity' and 'Lincredible', while Lindsey Vonn's success as the 2010 Olympics caused the host city to be dubbed 'Vonncouver'. These examples look pretty hackneyed and more contrived than creative. Although a boxer once described by a journalist as 'floating like a lead balloon and stinging like a dead bee', paraphrasing the famous quote of Muhammad Ali, is an example of more clever use of words.

Column writing

Many of those responsible for colour writing, usually the preserve of the chief sportswriter, also contribute regular opinion columns once or twice a week. Online they are often labelled as blogs but the content is the same. Columnists are the centre forwards of any sports desk – it's the glamour job, one of the hardest and one of the best remunerated. Much like players or athletes, columnists have to set a standard and maintain it. Many journalists could write one good column but repeating it week in, week out is an incredibly difficult task.

However, almost without exception the best sports columnists are, or have been, reporters. Sport is full of opinions – in pubs, on Twitter and on radio phone-ins. From the moment the whistle is blown, the hooter sounds or the final ball is struck, people have got something to say about what they've just witnessed. But there's a big difference between holding court at the bar and holding the attention of a reader. Patrick Collins, the *Mail on Sunday*'s five-time sportswriter of the year, claims if you don't grab a reader by the first two paragraphs they have probably already moved on to something else: 'You may choose an important subject and compose 1500 words of high-minded prose, but if the reader isn't grabbed within the first two paragraphs, then you've wasted your time.'

You will see a common theme developing in match featuring, profiles, features, interviews, colour writing and now columns. The introduction is everything. If you carried out a time-and-motion study on most journalists, you would see they spend a huge percentage of the total time it takes to compose a story, writing, deleting, tweaking, polishing, deleting again and then rewriting again their first paragraph. After you've nailed that all important opening, the rest should flow, in theory.

Content for opinion columns is often driven from the sporting agenda but they can also cast light on a cause or a little-reported incident that needs wider exposure. Columnists see it as their responsibility to set the agenda rather than slavishly follow it. Good columnists see or hear things that others miss and then have the ability to convey that information in a way that will interest the reader. They have to be original too. A column can focus on recent events but it needs to give a new insight, although they rarely tend to break news. They can be made up of a single piece or a lead item and two to three small items. Some columnists also work with a cartoonist to illustrate their work.

Most columnists don't worry about being popular – a string of negative comments or an email inbox full of angry emails is much better than your copy provoking absolutely no reaction. 'Paul Dacre understands his market better than any rival,' said *Daily Mail* sports columnist Des Kelly of his editor. 'The day I joined, he said, "Make them laugh, make them cry, or make them angry", which isn't a bad template for a columnist.'

Ghosting

In addition to opinion columns, most publications, online and offline, use former players or athletes to give their views in first-person pieces published under their own byline. In reality, few of these former sports stars actually write the pieces themselves. Instead, they are assigned a reporter who interviews them about a topic – usually the two might decide in advance what could be good material – and then craft their answers into a column that is then sent back for approval. This is known as 'ghosting' and it's vitally important that the athlete and the journalist develop a close relationship. The former stars are trusting their voice and reputation to their ghosts, but the journalists know they need to produce a story and too often people once involved in sport are reticent to criticise because they still have close friends involved.

In addition to former players and athletes, some still competing provide columns. Austin Healey found himself in hot water during the 2001 Lions rugby tour for his ghosted column. His ghostwriter even sprung to his defence at a later disciplinary hearing, but Healey was ruled responsible for the contents of the article and heavily fined. The use of sporting names to write for newspapers is nothing new – Donald Bradman wrote extensively during his cricketing career and publications like to be able to tease and trumpet that a big name writes exclusively for them. However, increasingly, teams have banned their players and athletes from contributing to newspapers during major competitions, with the danger something could be said that could divide the camp or unnecessarily inspire competition or rivals.

Ben Baker, who graduated from his NCTJ journalism training at News Associates three years ago and is responsible for former footballer Andy Gray's syndicated column at press agency Sportsbeat, said:

> The quicker you form a good relationship with the person you are ghosting the better. They need to be able to trust that you will portray them well, make them sound authoritative and erudite. I normally send across an email with some talking points and then call 24 hours later. Sometimes the angle is very obvious but it's not always, and usually this makes for a better column. If you have something controversial it's always worth double-checking it and running it by your columnist, just to make sure they are happy with how you've phrased it.

In addition to opinion and personality columns, newspapers and websites regularly run speciality features in which the subject matter is predetermined, either on a particular sport or facet of sport, such as television coverage. If you are the golf correspondent, you will produce your share of event reporting, quotes stories and features but a weekly or monthly column might allow you to go into more depth and cover a broader range of subjects not necessarily in the news.

Many newspapers appoint a sports diarist, whose job is to knit together a number of news stories, sometimes gossipy, sometimes newsy, into a regular bylined column. Usually, a diary is made up of four to six individual items that on their own aren't substantial enough to make a news story. Diarists can wield a tremendous amount of influence within sport and they are frequently the first thing those in the industry read and their stories are widely followed up. At major events, diaries are often produced to give a background flavour to the competition and cover stories that don't make it into news, feature and colour reports.

Below is an example of a diary produced during Wimbledon named 'Court Circular'. On their own, none of these stories are strong enough to demand space but they can be knitted together to provide a different take on what goes on behind the scenes.

All England Club regular Sir Cliff Richard happily snapped away with his camera as Centre Court's new roof was closed. But away from his beloved Wimbledon, the 68-year-old crooner was having problems closer to home. Sir Cliff has been ordered to tear down a £30,000 conservatory at his £3 million home in Virginia Water, Surrey. All England Club officials are used to planning wrangles with local Merton council but it seems Sir Cliff had no permission for the appendage to his kitchen.

Wimbledon groundsman Eddie Seaward reached retirement age in January but the man responsible for SW19's flawless manicured lawns has been asked to stay on for another three years. The club are facing one of their greatest challenges when staging the tennis at the London 2012 Olympics and Eddie Seaward's successor will, in less than a month, return the courts to pristine condition after Wimbledon. Seaward joined the All England Club in 1990 and received the 2008 Lifetime Achievement Award at the Turf Professional Awards.

Serena Williams is the top tennis Twitterer [sic] – with nearly half a million followers. This week sister Venus has opened an account but she's lagging behind in the popularity stakes, she's only got 1 per cent of that number. Mind you, her tweets are hardly insightful. Take this: 'Hello everyone, today was a good day at the tennis.' Fascinating.

The BBC has dismissed claims they had any major say over the timing of Andy Murray's appearances to increase their ratings. The BBC One audience for his five-set victory over Switzerland's Stanislas Wawrinka peaked at 12.6 million, more than half of the television share that night. The average audience between 6.30 p.m. and 10.40 p.m. registered at 8.1 million as Murray battled to secure his place in the quarter finals. But a spokeswoman said they had applied no pressure on the Championships. 'The BBC – along with all the other broadcasters on site – put in a request for their preference order of players,' she said.

Wimbledon favourite Roger Federer has grown tired of answering the 'questioners' at his post-match press conferences and has decided to communicate with his legion of fans via Facebook. The five-times champ posted a message saying he will do his best to answer questions from fans, seeing as he spent so much time chinwagging with the SW19 journos. Within an hour he had more than 20,000 responses. Sheng Yang from Taiwan clearly has designs on being Federer's dietician. 'Hello! Do you like to eat fruit? There is a lot of litchi (lychee) in my country.

If you have a free time, welcome to my country.' While question of the day goes to Mostafezur Rahman: 'Whenever it comes to your mind that you are Roger Federer, how do u feel?'

9

BIG STORY

NEWS GATHERING, SOURCES AND CONTACTS

Most editors make a simple demand of their reporters – 'Tell me something I don't already know.' But this is pretty hard when every sports event, from the high profile to the obscure, is broadcast live and results whizz around the globe within seconds.

Sport is big money. Premier League clubs have combined annual revenues approaching £3 billion while some estimate the 2022 FIFA World Cup will cost more than £138 billion to stage. Sport is big business. The International Olympic Committee (IOC) and football's world governing body FIFA have major brands lining up to contribute over £1 billion in marketing rights, while American broadcaster NBC recently paid £2.7 billion to broadcast the 2014, 2016, 2018 and 2020 Olympic Games. Sport is big politics. Just witness the world leaders queuing up to help secure their countries major events – Tony Blair, Barack Obama and Vladimir Putin have all made time in their schedules for politicking at sporting gatherings. When these three combine there are, inevitably, big stories.

For many years, sports journalists have had a reputation for keeping breaking news to themselves, which is probably why they were viewed with such suspicion by their colleagues in news. There are numerous tales of journalists sitting on stories during major tournaments or sports tours because they wanted to remain on the inner circle. However, with the advent of a non-stop news media, with 24/7 sports channels hungry for content and websites and newspapers operating in an environment in which they know sports sell, the previous cosy culture has changed.

In the past, many of the major news stories involving sport were broken by those operating in news. In the mid-1960s, *Sunday People* investigative journalist Michael Gabbert, uncovered a betting scandal in English football that lead to eight players being imprisoned. Andrew Jennings, like Gabbert, was not a regular in press boxes but still used his connections in the corridors of sporting power to break a series of stories about corruption at IOC and FIFA. He has been highly critical about how sports journalists have been reporting stories of corruption at the world's two most powerful sporting organisations.

Jennings cites a column written by the *Mail on Sunday*'s chief sportswriter Patrick Collins in the days after England received just two votes in their bid to host the 2018 World Cup. Collins wrote that he had attended a private dinner, with three or four other journalists earlier that year, in which the bid-team leader had said 'at least 13' voting members of FIFA's executive committee were 'buyable'. Collins claimed the journalists sat on the information because to report the comments would have ruined any hopes England had of staging the tournament, a reality of the job but one that doesn't help shed the 'fans with typewriters' image often applied to sportswriters. 'Aware of the stakes, we swallowed hard and respected the confidence' he wrote. After England lost, the British media widely rounded on FIFA, accusing their rivals of wrongdoing, which Jennings claimed was too late and made them complicit to the corruption:

> There are some very good reporters around but they don't seem to work in sports news. It's time editors started looking at the garbage that you get from sports news reporters. They are probably the worst in the world. They won't check, they won't research and they won't cultivate the sources that you need to get the documents that reveal what is really going on.

Another major sports news story – broken by the no-longer published *News of the World* about match fixing in cricket – was also produced by those working on specialist investigation teams with no direct involvement in sports reporting. The investigation had an enormous budget, which would probably be enough to finance a major sports desk's overseas travel budget for an entire year. Of course, these stories have been widely followed up by sports journalists, who have often, using their contacts, revealed further details in follow-ups but the allegation is they didn't lead from the front.

Jennings's criticism does seem a little unfair. Sports journalists are not afforded the time to spend weeks or months investigating a story. They must attend events, write previews, secure interviews and still break their own stories, although perhaps these don't require the months of time-consuming, and therefore very expensive investigation, work to produce – and remember that many investigations don't ever get published or broadcast. In today's multimedia age, this workload has only increased. Journalists on most newspapers now file repeatedly for their publication's website and newspaper. Newspapers now consider themselves media owners as much as publishers.

There is more competition for news. A press conference that was once held for a handful of journalists who all had the luxury of filing for the next day's newspaper, now has a chance of being broadcast live. If not, press agencies and wire services will distribute the best angles within minutes – which will be syndicated to hundreds of websites around the world instantly. If the press conference is held at 11 a.m., it is nearly a day before the newspaper journalists get their story in print – by which time the story has already moved on. It means they probably have to dig around harder for material than ever before.

In the past, if journalists received a tip about a hot news story, they would face the challenge of standing it up – checking out the validity of the information with sources and contacts and then having the anxiety of hoping no one else caught wind of their exclusive before their publication date. Now most newspaper journalists have the ability to publish online if they fear others are closing in on their scoop, although most would admit they get extra satisfaction, and credit, from keeping their news exclusive until the printed product hits the streets.

Much sports news happens 'on diary', that is it is known about in the form of a press conference, media briefing or an annual general meeting. But being able to work 'off diary', to set rather than follow the agenda, is a skill prized by all editors. That comes from anticipating what might happen, working with contacts or keeping an ear to the ground for rumour or gossip that with hard work could become a hard news story. Newsgathering is not easy. Developing a news sense is caught not taught, but despite Jennings's criticism, sports journalists produce more quality news content than ever before – especially as they have more space to fill, both online and in print.

Cultivating contacts

Covering what happens on the field of play is just a small part of a sports journalist's job. Those at the top of it almost without exception have developed and cultivated the best contacts. Journalists must be conduits for a constant source of information – from rival media, official communications and close contacts. The majority of sports journalists graduate to their positions from working in other departments, principally news, and the rules for good sports journalism are the same as journalism in general. And all journalists will tell you that the most valuable item in their toolkit is their contacts book.

When you start out as a journalist, every person you come into contact with could become a contact. Say you regularly cover a non-league football club and interview their captain and develop a good relationship with him. That team might then enjoy a run in the FA Cup and suddenly become big news because they've got a plum third round against Manchester United at

Old Trafford. Suddenly the semi-pro defender you used to interview will be marking Wayne Rooney and, for a brief spell, become an in-demand interviewee. But you are the one he trusts. He's more likely to speak to you over the others and give you better material. So set about building this contact book from day one. Sometimes people are reticent to give away personal details, such as mobile telephone numbers, but are happy to share email addresses – although phone calls are much more difficult to ignore than emails. You should always finish interviews by asking for a contact number should you have any follow-up questions. Besides, if you phrase your request like, 'If when I transcribe this interview anything isn't clear or I want to check something can I give you a call?', interviewees are more likely to share their contact details with you. After all, it's in their interest to make sure their comments are as accurately reported as possible.

Contacts are nurtured over time and can be a valuable commodity, with journalists often moving to better roles on the strength of their contacts book. However, be realistic. If you are doing an interview with a big-name Premier League player, he is unlikely to give you this information just minutes after he's met you. He is more likely to refer you to his agent or the press department of his club or national team. Some journalists do become friends with those they regularly interview but don't confuse sharing confidences and gossip with true friendship – in today's media it doesn't tend to happen. Being friendly but not considering yourself a friend might be the best approach in the majority of cases. Lee Mottershead of the *Racing Post* offers the following advice about contacts:

> Contacts are immensely important, but more critical is not so much the contacts you have but the relationship you have with them. It is not hard to get someone's mobile number or to shake their hand. Much more difficult is reaching the stage where the contact feels sufficiently comfortable to talk with you on and off the record. Build that sort of relationship and you will often stay one step ahead of the game and find yourself made aware of stories before others. Moreover, as a person becomes comfortable with a journalist he or she will tell friends and your contacts book will grow ever larger.

So gaining contacts can be relatively easy, knowing how to cultivate them – when to use them and when not to use them – is much harder. Sometimes, you might even have a story that you know may really irritate or anger a key contact and this is always a tough call to make. Sportsbeat's executive editor David Parsons recalls:

I remember interviewing a very senior administrative official, who had just been appointed as chief executive to one of the big national governing bodies. During the course of a lively and free-flowing conversation, he veered on and off the record. When I transcribed the notes, it was unclear whether one fairly powerful set of quotes he gave me was for publication or background. It would have made a nice story, but I took the decision that cultivating the contact was more important – especially as he was new to the role and burning my bridges for a good but not great copy didn't make sense. I rang him to seek clarification, which he was very grateful for. I missed out on a story, but I got many more out of him in the long run because I'd established myself as someone who he could trust.

Developing contacts is becoming harder to do when the pace of journalism is becoming more and more unremitting, with a demand for constant copy too often keeping reporters tied to their desks and reliant on their telephones. However, where possible you should get out and meet people face to face. You don't always meet a contact to guarantee a story. Sometimes, it will be a mutual exchange of gossip over a coffee or a drink. You might be given a tip about a story but will have to use other contacts to stand it up. One of the great frustrations of journalism is the amount that you know but can't write – either because of legal issues, the fact it is gossip that can't be proven or you've been told information off the record.

You will rely on those who work in press departments and PR agencies in the same way they will rely on you. However, it's worth remembering that when you are starting out and don't have any contacts, they will control your access. So make a good impression and try your best to make them like you. They should understand that you might occasionally write things they would rather were not printed, but if you are seen as a straight and fair operator it will help. If a new press manager has been appointed to a club, team or event, drop them a note, arrange to meet for a coffee to introduce yourself – don't expect them to court you, it works both ways. Equally, don't always have an ulterior motive for ringing a contact. Sometimes it's just good to touch base and check in. It also pays to drop a text or an email after a good achievement or to wish luck ahead of a major event. Developing contacts can be time-consuming but can also pay dividends.

Some journalists also use Twitter as a way of developing contacts. For example, 'Good to catch up with @J_Ennis today, have a safe flight out to Doha,' or 'Congratulations to @J_Ennis on her long jump personal best, looking forward to catching up soon.' However, remember your rivals are following too. Do you want them to know you've got an interview running or any advance preview of a story you have? When you are interviewing someone, it is important that you tell them that you are a journalist and that his or her comments will be reported. There are, of course, exceptions. Sometimes, for an investigation, such as the cricket match-fixing story, revealing you are a reporter would scupper any hopes of gaining the evidence you need to publish.

Off the record

As a journalist, you will need to understand how to deal with 'off the record' conversations, which certainly becomes easier with experience. You will often be told something on a background basis. Sometimes this information might not be for publication. Sometimes you are given it on the understanding that it cannot be attributed.

Sources 'close' to a player might be the player's agent or even the player. An 'unnamed' team official might be a senior coach or media official. It's a truth that 'friends of United manager Joe Smith' almost always means Joe Smith himself. Sometimes you might be told something a person says that they don't really want you to report, which actually they really do want you to report. They just don't want to say it. It's a confusing business reading between the lines but if in doubt seek clarification. In addition, it's always worth making sure both sides know the guidelines by which information is being provided.

Protecting off-the-record confidences is key to building up a contacts book and protecting your sources – never revealing or betraying those who have confided in you – is one of the basic conditions for press freedom. However, with all of the above it is always worth remembering that you are there to report, even if that means upsetting someone. It's a problem more acutely felt by reporters who cover the same team and athletes week in, week out on the beat. Be too critical and you might lose access, but be not critical enough and readers will soon write you off as being 'in the pocket' of those you report on.

Sometimes journalists' opinions are sought out by club officials. Perhaps they might be asked what gossip they've heard around a certain player and whether he is in transfer talks with other clubs. Occasionally, journalists have acted as intermediaries in transfer deals on the understanding they will receive privileged information in the future, perhaps a heads-up on their rivals before a story breaks.

In football, it's probably more useful to have good relationships with agents than the players themselves. Agents and players have a symbiotic relationship and agents use this access to information to their advantage. If you want to know the mood of a dressing-room after a run of defeats, an agent who represents a key player at that club would be a good starting point. However, remember agents sometimes use the media to their own advantage. For example, if one club is stalling on personal terms of a new contract it could be beneficial to them for that player to be suddenly linked to another club in a bid to shift negotiations along.

Off the field – what else you'll need to know

So much of sport is no longer about what happens on the field of play. Indeed what happens off the field of play can frequently be more interesting and it gives the journalist the chance to tell readers something they didn't know. A sports journalist needs to be able to read and understand a balance sheet – vital following the introduction of financial fair play regulations or working out whether a cash-strapped club can pay the interest on their debts. A journalist needs to understand business – the difference between a limited company and a public limited company (PLC), what occurs at a shareholders' meeting and explain what happens when a business goes into administration. A journalist must be an aspiring medic – do you know the difference between an anterior and posterior cruciate ligament or the performance-enhancing capabilities of erythropoietin?

Legal knowledge is also key to any journalist. Sports stars can find themselves in court on a range of charges and knowing what you can and can't say when reporting these cases is very important. Get it wrong and you could find yourself held in contempt – which carries far stricter sanctions than getting a scoreline incorrect. The trial of former Leeds United footballers Jonathan Woodgate and Lee Bowyer, who had been accused of grievous bodily harm, collapsed after a newspaper printed an interview with the father of the alleged victim, while the jury considered its verdict. The newspaper in question was ordered to pay £175,000 in fines and costs – an expensive mistake after which the editor resigned.

More and more journalists are live tweeting during court cases, although this practice remains at the discretion of the judge, but they must be aware of the information they can and cannot publish. During the trial of Tottenham Hotspur manager Harry Redknapp for tax evasion, one reporter found himself in trouble after he tweeted the name of a juror and also reported the evidence of a witness given under oath when the jury was not present.

Tweets should relate to factual matters only – such as reporting what has been said in court or what stage the trial has reached. They should never contain the reporter's comments on the evidence, for example, 'The witness is buckling under cross-examination', or 'The jury does not seem to be impressed by this evidence.' It is argued that such comments undermine the defendants' right to receive a fair trial. Contractual disputes also get decided in civil court so a sports journalist might find themselves attending an inquest or an employment tribunal. In addition, next to stars of entertainment, sports stars and administrators are known to be regular and sometimes serial litigants. Some football club chairmen are even known to do it for sport.

As a journalist, often your job is to write stories that will annoy those in positions of power and responsibility – a legal threat need not force you into a hasty retreat. Remember the defence of fair comment applies to comment pieces only and a defamatory statement is one that could cause someone to be shunned or avoided, expose them to hatred, ridicule or contempt, disparage a person in their trade or profession or lower a person in the estimation of right-thinking members of society. Now take into account all the above and imagine you are writing a news follow-up to a disastrous England penalty shoot-out performance in the second round of the World Cup. However, if you've got your information right and you've presented it to withstand legal challenge, then there should be no cause for concern.

Most respected journalism courses spend plenty of time on the complex issues surrounding media law and the recommended text remains the most up to date version of *McNae's Essential Law for Journalists*. Of course all news stories must be accurate and contain enough context in the story to ensure balance and fairness. You should give those you write about appropriate time for a right of reply, although journalists will always fear that as soon as they reveal the material they are working on, the story could be lost from their control. It's also not unknown for clubs or athletes, knowing a publication has what they conceive to be a negative story about to run, to get their side of the story out first by going to a rival publication, which will portray them in a more sympathetic light.

Knowing how sports are administered and funded is vital – a decision that football's world governing body FIFA take in Geneva affects football from the parks to the Premiership. It is increasingly those in suits, rather than tracksuits, that have the biggest say on how sport is administered. International sports federations, national governing bodies, media owners – who contribute millions in rights – club owners and management are all sources that have to be cultivated. As do funding agencies and government departments responsible for sports policy, from grass sports to elite level. Sports Accord is an annual gathering of all the world's leading sports administrators and a rich mine of stories, while SoccerEx is another event in which leading officials from clubs and organisations such as FIFA and UEFA come to do business.

Club coaches and managers change with regularity – in English football's second flight, managers are dismissed after an average of 1.2 seasons in charge. So if you regularly cover the same club, by the time you've won the manager's confidence he might well be packing his bags. Therefore, senior management, such as the chairman, chief executive or club secretary, are important people to have as contacts, because they are likely to be around longer.

Sports journalists often work alongside their counterparts in other fields, such as finance, business, royal, politics and entertainment, in addition to general assignment news reporters on coverage. Nowhere was this more true than in the build-up to the London 2012 Olympics, a £9.3-billion project that had as many news angles as sporting ones. In addition, many publications now employ sports news correspondents who report to the news desk rather than the sports editor; their focus is less on what happens on the field of play, although that sometimes drives the agenda, and more on the news behind the scenes – everything from a new sponsorship deal to allegations of corruption.

Some basic rules

Every publication, whether it is online or offline, has its own style guide and story construction should always be considered with this in mind. Editors have pet hates – for example, the use of the word 'brace', a very old shooting term for two, when 'double' is much more widely understood. However, if you follow some of the basic rules below for news writing, you won't go far wrong and, with experience, you will start to realise how these can be bent and adapted:

- Each paragraph should generally be a sentence of 25 words maximum – rarely if ever have more than 25 in the first paragraph. Get the key lines in, but, if you can do it tightly enough, your first paragraph could easily be 20 words or less for better impact.
- International news agency Reuters issue this advice to their news journalists: 'If there are more than 25, start to get nervous. If there are more than 30 then get very nervous. By the time you reach 40 it's time to break the sentence in two and reach for a full stop.'
- The introduction is crucial – the most important sentence – and must be crystal clear, snappy, straight down the line and just one sentence. Tell the reader immediately what has happened and get across why it's important. If you haven't told the story in the first two paragraphs, then it's too late.

- Don't waste words anywhere and never repeat yourself – words are a precious commodity for a journalist. You will almost always have more information that you want to write about than space you are given.
- Avoid hyperbole, 'criticised' is better than 'slammed' or 'blasted'. 'Begged' or 'pleaded' is okay in a hostage situation but not for a story about increased season-ticket prices. In general, 'urged' or 'called for' also work but remain accurate and steer clear of anything over the top.
- As with match reporting, impact starts are crucial so avoid a delayed impact, which is fine for features, for example, 'On a cold and blustery winter morning ...' – get to the point straight away.
- Remember the pub test. Imagine reading your story out loud to your friends. Do you write as you would say it? Use choice wording that is economical and easy on the eye.
- Too many trainee journalists trip themselves up over the use of tenses – 'has been' and 'have been' are generally seen as vague and weak. Use them if you absolutely have to – if you are unsure when something happened – but avoid them if at all possible. If you know when something happened you should be able to use the present or the past tense. So, 'was stabbed' is better than 'has been stabbed', 'is recovering' is better than 'has been recovering' etc. Crucially, whatever you do, don't change the meaning, but, where applicable, putting something in the present tense makes it more immediate (a good thing). Therefore, 'is distraught' is better than 'was distraught last night' – which could imply the person in question was upset but isn't any more.
- Try to get a name in the first paragraph whenever possible. How you present it depends on how well known the person is. For example, 'Manchester United manager Sir Alex Ferguson believes television has too much power over football after the Premier League signed their first ever £2 billion rights deal.' Do you need Manchester United manager? Isn't he well known enough to avoid this? You could also drop this in further down your story, for example in a second paragraph that read: 'Manchester United's manager wants the Premier League to stand up to their broadcast paymasters, who want to introduce live games on Friday nights, which could cause major fixture congestion for those involved in European campaigns.'
- Background facts like age should generally not appear in your first paragraph unless they are key to the story – for example, 'A 95-year-old will run with the Olympic torch,' or 'A 17-year-old drops dead of heart attack while running a half marathon.' Use your news sense.

- If a person, place or an organisation is relatively unknown, generally don't use their names in your first paragraph because it causes clutter. Summarise who it is in the first paragraph and name it properly in the second or third. For example, 'Paul Deighton, the chief executive officer of the London Organising Committee of the Olympic and Paralympic Games, has urged ticket holders …' has no impact. Deighton might be well known to journalists but not to the average reader and you are 20 words in before you get near the story. 'Olympic ticket holders have been urged …' is better and more snappy but it's still a bit passive and the 'have been' is weak. 'Olympic organisers have urged ticket holders' is an improvement, this intro is already more active. 'Olympic organisers are urging' is much better – it is more like the story is happening right now, which makes it seem more relevant. The present tense improves your story, where justified. Likewise, when summarising, you might refer to the chief executive officer of the London Organising Committee of the Olympic and Paralympic Games as 'Olympic organisers' in the first paragraph. You can use Deighton's exact title later on but don't clutter your first paragraph with it.

Names and titles

In news pages, you would call someone 'John Smith' first then 'Mr Smith' thereafter; likewise 'June Smith' and then 'Mrs Smith' or 'Miss Smith'. However, you would never use titles with full names – so don't write 'Mrs June Smith'. For sports stories, however, it is standard convention to drop the courtesy title – Mr or Mrs – and just say 'Smith' from the second time onwards. For children or if you really want to help create a friendly or light-hearted tone, give the full name first (no Mr, Mrs or Miss), and use just the first name thereafter. If someone has been knighted, call him 'Sir John Smith' first, then 'Sir John' afterwards. However, by contrast, it's 'Lord John Smith' and thereafter 'Lord Smith'. An organisation can be called 'they' if already named – assuming it's clear what you are talking about. Some sports sections have taken the decision, considering the number of sports stars, retired or still active, with honorific titles to name them in full at the first mention – like 'Sir Chris Hoy' or 'Lord Seb Coe' and then just use the surname, 'Hoy' or 'Coe', subsequently. Sporting honours don't need to be mentioned either; for example you don't need to write 'Olympic champion Amy Williams MBE'. However, it will do you no harm to seek advice from your editor or publication about how titles are used. It will show that you understand the editorial process.

- Wherever possible, use pretty much every fact available to you. If you write tightly enough, which is key, you should be able to get more or less everything in. However, there may be occasions when you are really tight or given a barrage of facts on one particular topic, such as loads of stats to demonstrate how women's attendance at football matches has risen in the last year or how sports participation among a certain age group has declined. In these cases, you may be able to pick and choose a bit, but don't leave too much out. It goes without saying, leave out the background information – not the crux of the story.

Who, what, where, how, when and why

In news stories – the *who, what, where, how, when* and *why* – are important. These are generally seen as the key ingredients – all six are vital and should almost always appear before your quotes. In an ideal world, you could get all six into the first paragraph but realistically this feat is unlikely but don't panic, it is no big deal. The key is to get them in approximate order of importance without repeating yourself or waffling – and to avoid anything that looks like your own opinion. There may be no magic order, but your news sense will help you decide. In general, *who* and *what* should be in your top paragraph. *Where* and *when* are also vital. They will very often be in your first paragraph but should be included further down if they detract from the story – for example, if an event happened four weeks ago or a few miles away. *How* and *why* (which expand on the *who* and *what*) might be dropped into paragraph two or three a bit more often. None of this is set in stone though.

- There may be two or more key angles you are mulling over, in which case get them all in the first three paragraphs. The marking guides stipulate all key lines must be high up. You may have some choice about which to stick in your top paragraph but the guide will always stipulate certain things that really should be in the top three.
- You will often encounter long-winded titles and may occasionally have to make a judgement call on whether to give someone his or her full title. For example, Sir Clive Woodward is the British Olympic Association's Director of Elite Performance. Sir Clive Woodward's business card reads Director of Elite Performance, British Olympic Association. By the time you include his name and job title, this amounts to ten words. If you can simplify a title without trivialising it, you may be able to abbreviate a little but don't take liberties – you'd have to be certain you are not changing the meaning. You may encounter jargon, for example Blackburn Rovers'

home games are formally policed by the Lancashire Constabulary but most readers would know them as Lancashire police.

- Another element of news writing many trainee reporters get wrong is confusing their singulars and plurals. You can refer to many organisations, such as the Football Association, a supporters' association or an athletics club in either the singular or plural but you must stick to it and be consistent throughout your reports. Do not say, for example, 'British Swimming *is* planning to raise *their* performance standards.' The 'is' refers to the organisation as a singular body but the 'their' refers to it as a plural collection of people, hence it is confused. You would need to say either, 'British Swimming *is* planning to raise *its* performance standards,' or 'British Swimming *are* planning to raise *their* performance standards.' Likewise, don't write, 'The club *is* bidding to extend *its* ground,' and then write '*They* want to build …' Make up your mind – singular or plural – and stick with it.

- Much like all other forms of journalism, you must avoid clichés.

- The word 'local' is ambiguous and usually frowned upon. Try not to use it and only do so if you have clearly identified the locals you are referring to.

- Either 'more than' or 'over' can be used when talking about numbers and statistics but again, pick one and be consistent in your pieces.

- Numbers are used regularly in sports journalism and each publication will have a style for this. Some spell out 1 to 10, but others only applies this for 1 to 9. For example, 'British Cycling will send a nine-strong squad to the first World Cup meeting of the season. It is not, 'British Cycling will send a 9-strong squad to the 1st World Cup meeting of the season.' When using numbers above 9 or 10, depending on guidance, then numerals are preferred. It's the '30th Olympic Games' not the 'Thirtieth Olympic Games' and the winning goal was scored in the '47th minute' not the 'forty-seventh minute'. However, if you want to start a sentence with a number, spell it out; for example, 'Twelve children died in a freak accident' – but avoid starting with numbers above 20.

- Write in an appropriate tone. If it is a funny story, then a light-hearted approach is great, but the chances are even if you find a story about a figure skater slipping over and breaking his leg amusing – newsrooms tend to boast about their own dark humour after all – the readers won't, so always be tactful.

- Avoid anything that looks like your own opinion – you won't have room for it anyway. There is a place for it in match reporting, features and certainly columns, but news writing should always be balanced. However, there is nothing wrong with the occasional word to add spice if it is obviously justified. In a piece with the headline 'Conmen trick supporters of a cash-strapped amateur sports club into believing they are wealthy benefactors', you can certainly refer to the confidence tricksters as 'callous', 'heartless' or 'mean'.

- When presenting quotes, mix direct quotations with reported speech. Emotive quotes can make copy but don't drag on for ages unless necessary. Generally speaking, if it can run as a fact, you don't need it as a quote. If someone is merely explaining something, it is much better in your own words, not quoted.

- Avoid half quoting, or running into your quotes; for example:

    He said it was a 'sad day for English cricket'.

    This is seen as sloppy.

    He said: 'It was a sad day for English cricket.'

    This is far better. He said, colon, quote – with the full stop inside the quote marks at the end. The only other way is to attribute at the end of the quote, like so:

    'Pick some quotes here,' he said. 'And you can also add some more of his quotes picked from anywhere else right here if you wish.'

    Full stops and commas are inside quote marks and in this second case 'he' does not have an initial capital letter.

- Obviously it is important to quote accurately, although it is possible to remove pauses and repetition and tidy up the quotes, providing you don't change the meaning. For example, if the directly transcribed quote is, 'I'm really, quite delighted, really delighted to receive this award. It's great to get recognition. Recognition is really special when it comes from your peers.' This could become, 'I'm delighted to receive this award. Recognition from your peers is really special.'

- It is important that you are consistent with the tenses in your reported speech. So if it *was* [past tense] a lovely day yesterday, use 'said' [past tense]. Likewise, 'He *says* [present tense] it *is* [present tense] a lovely day today,' is correct. Your best bet is to use 'said', 'added' or 'explained' to introduce past-tense reported speech but to stick to 'says' (not 'adds' or 'explains') if you want the paragraph to be in the present or future tense

('He says it will be a lovely day tomorrow' is correct). In addition, when using reported speech, try to avoid any words that confuse the tenses – for example, words like would, could, may, has and has been.

- News now happens at pace, but accuracy should always be prized and never sacrificed for speed. Double-check facts, figures, names, dates and spellings and have a well-trained eye for typos. Read over your first draft and look to tighten up your writing – can that 25-word sentence be condensed to just a few words? Do paragraphs four and five say virtually the same thing? Words are a precious commodity – you never have enough – so avoid any superfluousness that doesn't add to the story. The more words you save, the more detail you can dress back in.

10

BIG CHANGES

WE'RE ALL MULTIMEDIA JOURNALISTS NOW

Print journalists, radio journalists and television journalists – the old demarcation lines that separated them have gone forever and we're all multimedia journalists now. Many old hands certainly aren't comfortable with the changes. They prefer copy to content and would rather refer to a newspaper as a publication rather than a media platform. However, just as print journalists have spent the last 50 years embracing changes and challenges, so they will again.

It is now not uncommon for a reporter to attend an event, conduct an interview on camera for a video package and then provide separate copy for use online and in a printed product. So it's as equally important to be well versed in developing technologies as it is in media law and shorthand. The internet has revolutionised the job of sports journalism – it has made it much easier and much harder in equal measure.

First, technology has made journalists more productive. There are millions of pages of research at your fingertips, allowing you to work quicker and more efficiently than ever before. It's easier to file and the internet gives journalists the luxury of unlimited space to develop stories, perhaps go into deeper background detail, which is something that doesn't exist in newspapers. And if you've got a red-hot story that you're worried will break or be revealed by a rival before your print deadline, you can sling it online and sit back while your rivals do the chasing.

As a journalist, you also want your work to be seen by the widest possible audience. In the past, the reach of a UK regional or even national title was limited, but now material is online it can be accessed from around the world. And those who claim that yesterday's news is tomorrow's fish-and-chips wrapping have been silenced by Google searches and extensive newspaper archives, all preserved online for posterity.

Recent NCTJ graduate Tom Barclay, who works for the *Sun*, where a reporter's story goes into a central copy basket and can easily find itself in the paper or online, says:

One of the great things with online is that it has limitless space. When I interviewed Olympic hurdler Dai Greene recently, it made about seven paragraphs in the paper. But the full interview, which was more than 500 words, was published online. Online articles can be more interactive. Readers can leave their comments, and with social networking, they can 'Like' it on Facebook and send it out via Twitter. This is great for journalists because it can send their story out to a wider audience.

I admit I was sceptical about Twitter when it first came along. Send a text message out to the whole world – how self-obsessed do you have to be to do that, and who's going to care? But from a journalist's point of view, Twitter is an essential tool for getting your story out there. The beauty of tweets and retweets means that your story can reach people who would never have read it had it been in the paper. The same goes for Facebook.

However, there is no textbook or course that can really be written to assist you in conquering this brave new world. By the time it's published or the syllabus is written, technology will have moved relentlessly on. So don't be a proud Luddite – embrace technology as part of your job, keep your knowledge up to date, look at what your rivals are doing and learn from them and, like journalists have since the invention of the printing press, just try and stay ahead of the game.

At the Beijing Olympics in 2008, Twitter users were posting 100 million tweets a quarter; four years later in London, this number had grown to 400 million a day. Indeed, usage spikes are often tied to prominent sporting events. Fans wrote nearly 3000 tweets per second during matches at the 2010 FIFA World Cup, while 7196 tweets per second were published during the 2011 FIFA Women's World Cup final between Japan and the USA.

Increased demands

If you were a journalist covering a leg of the Olympic torch relay in the build-up to the London 2012 Games, you might have needed more than a pen, paper and laptop. At any major event, the demands placed on journalists now have increased. You could be live tweeting off your smartphone and uploading pictures via Twitpic. You might need to be proficient in Audioboo to get short interview clips online or a live streaming website like Bambuser, while YouTube has turned everyone into a broadcaster competing for millions of eyeballs. A laptop and mobile phone with plenty of charge is vital when filing on the fly; indeed, back-up batteries are a must because there is no guarantee you will get close to a power source. If you do find a source, it will probably be taken, so make an extension lead part of your toolkit too. When it comes to writing your story, either for online or a more considered report, follow the photographers. They are experts at knowing where to file –and can normally be found in a good café with free Wi-Fi. However, despite all these advances and demands, the basics of reporting for the internet are no different. You need to tell the story quickly and with impact. According to Sportsbeat's executive editor David Parsons:

> I don't think our journalists do anything different when writing for a web client than they do if writing for a newspaper or magazine. Journalism is journalism no matter where it is printed. There is a massive priority to get stories out quickly online but striving to 'be the first' is nothing new. And sports journalists are used to these deadlines because even when they were working exclusively for newspapers, they were frequently filing when the paper was on deadline because of the nature of when sport takes place – in evenings or in different time zones.
>
> The biggest difference is probably with production, making sure stories are tagged with key words and the headline used is optimised for search engines. A newspaper headline on Jess Ennis winning gold at the Olympics might be 'Golden Girl' in 72-point type above a big picture of her holding her medal. Online it's more likely to be 'LONDON 2012: Golden girl Jess Ennis wins Olympic heptathlon' – it's more of a label than a headline, but it does the job. Headlines drive internet searches so what works in a paper must be reconsidered online. But new-age distractions – such as email, Facebook and instant messaging – make it harder to capture and, more importantly, hold the attention of your readers.

For several years the tactic was to keep stories short and snappy online. This was in the belief that readers didn't have the tolerance to scroll down big blocks of text and the hope that the copy would be a sufficient tease for them still to pay for their newspapers. However, there is evidence that long-form journalism can survive online, especially with advances in the way that content can be presented, such as on tablet devices. The younger generation of media consumers also has much more tolerance for reading text on computer screens. And while it's easy to say that people have declining attention spans and consume their media in bite-sized chunks, it is not necessarily true. Think back 20 years and look at the shape of the media.

Maybe people bought one daily newspaper and consumed a couple of biweekly or monthly magazines. There was a limited choice of radio stations and perhaps no more than a handful of television stations. The closest they came to consuming breaking news in written form were from now-forgotten services like Teletext or the BBC's Ceefax. Now look at today's constantly evolving media landscape – the specialist television channels, some screened exclusively online, the growth of digital radio, social media, ebooks and, of course, the internet.

Maths isn't normally a strong point of most journalists – unless they are being creative with their expenses – but logic tells you that the more opportunities that exist for content, the more that usage will spread and the amount of time that each opportunity gets dedicated to it will decrease. In truth, people are probably more engaged with media – and in turn sports journalism – than ever before, although journalists must now contend with news cycles that are measured in minutes rather than hours and race to get ahead of breaking news that develops at a breakneck speed. Journalists who have adapted best to the changes are those that have accepted they are no longer at the centre of conversation but just a part of it.

In the past, the general public were observers rather than participants. The closest they could come to a more involved position would be if they had a letter to the editor published. Journalists have not readily accepted the involvement of the man, or woman, on the street as part of the storytelling process – and the community aspect of journalism is only going to increase. Citizen journalism is viewed with suspicion and engaging with readers remains something that most reporters do under sufferance.

However, in an age when loyalty to one newspaper, perhaps the title your parents subscribed to and their parents before that, no longer exists. It is vital to develop and maintain a relationship with readers via online media. Whether that is responding or reacting to comments left on a story, inviting readers to help set questions ahead of a major interview – 'I'm off to meet the new Chelsea manager today, what's the first question you would like me to ask?' – or treating Twitter as a two-way conversation other than using it as just another forum for your work. Nowhere is this interaction with readers more evident than the trend to report breaking news or sporting events as they happen in the form of a live blog. Live blogs can be factual, statistical and results driven, or conversational and humorous, encouraging plenty of participation from readers who get to feel they are part of the sporting action. Blogging, or text commentary, gives the journalist the ability to share what's happening right now and offers readers the chance to immediately engage and even shape, the story.

Chatterboxing and live blogging

Commenting on events online or on social media, usually while watching them on television, is known as chatterboxing. It is a modern media phenomenon and is on the rapid increase. A 2012 poll suggested that a quarter of social media-savvy adults, aged under 35, watch a sporting event live, rather than on catch-up, because they enjoy being part of the related social-media chatter around it. It's no longer enough to talk with the friends around you. There's a worldwide web of followers to interact with. Of course, sports events have always been social affairs, but social atmospheres are now playing out online as well as offline. A good live blog will hunt out this audience and embrace it, weaving social-media contributions through editorial and embedding links directing readers to more in-depth content elsewhere on the host site.

Live blogging enables a publication to get a story moving almost immediately, adding depth and colour – such as multimedia, pictures, quotes or graphics – as it develops. Content does not go through a time-consuming production process, such as subediting. It is published by its author seconds after it's written. BBC Sport's website has pioneered live blogging of sports events – producing hundreds of hours and thousands of words of coverage a year from a range of events. A team of writers compiles the articles from a central base, where they can access news feed, television pictures, and other broadcast media, and stay in contact with their reporters on the scene. Hashtags, such as #bbcfootball, can be applied and Twitter can be monitored for interesting reader tweets that can be weaved into coverage.

Ryan Bangs, Sportsbeat's Olympics editor, said:

During the London 2012 Olympics we produced our syndicated live blog from a team based in our office. It's hard, bordering on the impossible, for reporters in the field to take responsibility for a live blog – first, they will be away from their laptop gathering quotes, and a good live blog should be constantly updating, and second they have other deadline pressures to meet. Live bloggers in the office can be across several television stations, the internet, Twitter etc. Reporters in the field will be focused just on their event. Back in the office we can always see a broader picture.

Although the office compiled the coverage, we used our reporters on the scene to add colour and detail you can only achieve by actually being at the event. For example, an amusing banner in the crowd or something that happened away from the camera, such as an athlete being consoled by their coach in the mixed zone. Reporters were also encouraged to Tweet a top-line quote when they received it but not an entire transcript of an interview because we wanted to save something back for web and newspaper clients.

Readers interaction is key to a successful live blog, which is effectively a rolling reporter's notebook presented in the order a story develops. However, while you are effectively publishing copy in chunks, don't forget the importance of accuracy; otherwise, you will soon lose credibility. It's an old truth in journalism that reputations take a long time to earn and can be lost with a single mistake. Of course a live blog is the first take on a developing story and you should always correct and clarify if you have made an error or omission. Opinion is fine and humour is key and ideally your writing should try to strike a conversational tone, without descending into a monologue. Invite questions from readers and ask in return, seek their advice and feedback, make them part of the story and effectively your co-authors. Many websites have software built into their content management systems to produce live blogs. Some reporters use web-based applications such as CoveritLive that can be inserted into any web page as easily as a hyperlink.

Another increasingly popular way of drawing readers in and making them involved is the hosting of live web chats – in which the general public take the role of interviewer. However, it's true that a web chat allows athletes to filter questions, picking and choosing the ones they want to tackle. Answers also tend to be short and lacking in detail and there is no option for journalists to follow-up. Increasingly, athletes are also using their Twitter accounts in a bid to bypass the media altogether and inviting questions from their followers under an agreed hashtag. Journalists will always monitor such chats for newsworthy material, but it's frustrating being on the outside of the process with no ability to influence the questioning.

Online publishing is a growth area, although the challenge of making money from content continues to defeat some of the media's biggest business brains. Currently readers don't expect to pay for web content but original journalism remains incredibly expensive to produce. However, newspapers and established publishers now compete with websites, some more professional than others, that cut and paste their work, rewrite or reword it, rarely attribute, and never link back to the original source. The internet has seen the birth of copyright theft on a grand scale – from text to pictures to moving images. Covering a big sports event, such as the Olympics or World Cup, is a costly business. Travel, accommodation, expenses and the reporter's salary soon add up and established publishers have yet to find a way to protect their copyright and intellectual property from those who seek to profit from it without contributing to the cost of delivering it.

Making the internet pay

Journalism remains divided about whether the internet should always be free or whether there should be a charge to access material. *The Times* put all its content behind a paywall and saw its traffic plummet. The paper, however, remains steadfast in its commitment to charge for content, in the belief it is the only way to make the internet pay. Others have moved to a 'freemium' model, whereby a number of articles a month can be accessed before a paywall is erected or whereby certain prized and exclusive content is only available with a subscription, while breaking news, which is widely available across the internet, is free to access.

However, the best way to monetise a website remains from unique visitors and the number of page impressions they make. In terms of page impressions, unique visitors are trumped by returning visitors, those with a loyalty to a site who are more likely to browse extensively across its slate of content and make more page impressions. A page view is the total number of times an individual page is visited by all users. Page views are triggered when a request for a web page is made by a web server and the requested page is delivered to a user's browser. Unique visitors report the number of different users that have visited your website pages and are tracked by a browser cookie and internet provider address. When a user visits a site for the first time a cookie is assigned to their browser and regardless of how many visits the user makes during the time period, it is still counted only once.

So while returning visitors generate more page impressions, advertisers will allocate money based on audience reach, which will be calculated by the number of eyeballs that look at a particular home page, web page or section. They therefore prize unique users above all others – it's better for them that 1000 different people visited a page once than 100 people visit it ten times. Advertisers will also ask other questions, such as how many returning visitors a website site, i.e. people who make that web address a regular destination for their news, and the length of time the average user spends on a web page. All these statistics are readily available to web publishers and will form a key part of their commercial planning.

But internet users are fickle. They may have a number of sites among their favorites but they will browse extensively. If they are looking for an item of sports news, they might use a search engine, navigate to a site they've never previously used, read the information and click away, never to return.

Websites therefore have to be designed to be as sticky as possible, trapping the reader when they arrive and presenting them with enough options that may pique their interest to look around.

Of course, the internet makes it easier for anyone to become a publisher and any aspiring journalist can use basic packages, such as WordPress, to create a web presence for his or her work. In addition, sports that previously found themselves fighting for newspaper coverage, now have a dedicated online space for their fans and followers. Niche publications can thrive like never before in this digital space, but finding ways to make content pay remains challenging.

In the early days of the internet, a newspaper website would contain all the stories written for the print edition with little or no changes. But most newspapers have now embraced the internet and their journalists are fully integrated, working online and in print and trying to serve both masters, despite their very different demands. British newspaper the *Guardian* has been at the heart of embracing the shift towards digital publishing, winning a series of industry awards largely due to the interaction it promotes between journalists and readers. It was one of the first newspapers to integrate comments into their live blogs and readers remain at the heart of their online content. During the 2010 FIFA World Cup, the paper even recruited a fans' network of 150 citizen journalists around the world, who tweeted, blogged and sent in pictures via Flickr, so that editors were in a unique position to tell readers, in print and online, about the global impact of the tournament.

Web-centric approach

Some publishers are even adopting a 'web-first' or 'web-centric' approach to organising their stories, which has been dubbed 'reverse publishing'. This means the first priority for reporters and editors is to report and produce text and multimedia stories for the web, before then focusing on a story for the print edition. The logic being that the web is where people go for breaking news and instant reaction, while in print there is space for a more considered and analytical approach. Put simply, online is where you go to find out what happened and print is where you find out what might happen next. However, the *Daily Mail* – the world's most visited newspaper website – has a totally different strategy. Its website benefits from association with the printed product, and uses its content heavily, but it has its own journalists and editors working totally separately from the newspaper staff.

Web publishers also know that readers want more than just the written word – hence the requirement for most graduate reporters to be able to contribute as both a text and video journalist. Video clips are exactly the sort of sticky content that keep readers on a website, while they are also easier to commercialise than text stories. From the expensive to the bargain basement, there are wide ranges of equipment and editing programmes available, although the basics for their use are often the same.

Kate Bamber, who graduated from her NCTJ qualification at News Associates and now works as a video journalist at the Press Association, says:

> The most important thing is to engage the viewer and tell the story without leaving any questions unanswered – just as you would do in print journalism. The key thing to remember with video is that it is all about telling a story with pictures. That might sound obvious, but as a result, the images come first and then the words – something that can be tricky to get used to if you are used to writing purely for print.
>
> There are different skills involved in both print and broadcast journalism, but the drive towards reporters being able to film, edit, write scripts and also file copy for the story is increasing. I believe this makes it crucial for new journalists to possess multiple skills in a very competitive workplace and be able to film as well as write.
>
> Like any other type of reporter, a video journalist needs an eye for a good story and the ability to tell it through both images and words. You need to decide what images tell the story best and get a variety of shots – knowing what looks good and being a bit creative can pay dividends. Patience is key as there is a lot of waiting around and a cool head under pressure is important as you may have to resolve problems if equipment fails. Sharp elbows also help if you ever find yourself stuck in a huge media scrum and you cannot leave without getting your shot. There is no room for being shy.

However, there are drawbacks to producing video and written work simultaneously, because if you put interviewees in front on a camera they tend to give very different answers from those they'd give if being interviewed by a print journalist, even if the questions are identical. It might be better to grab the sound bites you need for your video and then complete the interview in the old-fashioned way, with notepad and Dictaphone. The news industry is still finding its feet with regards to how to use video online. Originally, they invested heavily and aimed at high production values. Many online editors have now realised a simple approach is just as effective and speedy multimedia content is much more desired than a more polished product. They also don't want to watch a video online that says exactly the same thing as the story that runs alongside it – videos and text should complement each other, just like photos and text do.

A sports editor from a major UK daily title said:

> As a company, we invested thousands in video equipment and software while producing high-end multimedia output. It is also labour intensive and therefore resource heavy. With video, you can instantly see how much impact it's having with the readers because the number of views is very transparent. We've produced some great content, top stories, backed up with great pictures and slick editing. However, it was sometimes depressing to see this had only been viewed by a few thousand people and the effort to gain ratio isn't really sustainable.
>
> Still our biggest hit – bringing in 30 times more views than anything else we've ever produced – was a video of a famous footballer, now in his 70s, dancing with some cheerleaders. It was shot for a joke by a reporter on her mobile phone, she emailed it around, we slung it online and it went viral. The production values were zero, the camera was wobbling all over the place and it wasn't clear what the story was. And people loved it.

Journalists are now regulars on television and radio, which helps spread their name recognition and the influence of the publication they work for. Some newspapers have even started to interview their own staff – using their reputation as resident experts – about the backstory behind a news conference or major event. This is then run as a video alongside the written story.

Digital media – and constantly developing technology such as tablets – continue to open up new avenues for sports journalists. Anyone and everyone can be a journalist online. Websites like Bleacher Report utilise an army of citizen reporters and take them into battle with established news organisations on a daily basis – the site is now the fourth most popular sports destination on the web in the United States and its influence is growing. However, readers still want an inside steer from an authoritative source, in addition to expecting news to be available as it breaks and it to be complemented by a full multimedia package – audio, video and graphics.

No matter how advanced the technology gets and how outdated this chapter reads, sports journalism on the web will depend on getting the basics right, grabbing readers' attention, maintaining it and leaving them interested in reading more.

11
NEXT STEP

WORK EXPERIENCE, TRAINING, GETTING A JOB AND WORKING AS A FREELANCER

I always turn to the sport section first. The sport section records people's accomplishments; the front page nothing but man's failures.

Earl Warren

It's a nice sentiment but I don't think Senator Warren has been following or covering England's football team during nearly 50 years of under-achievement.

Journalists might rank alongside politicians, estate agents and bankers when it comes to public trust but jobs in the industry remain prized – and few industries are more competitive. It's sobering to know there are more people graduating from media-related courses than there are jobs in the entire UK media and sports journalism remains probably the most popular specialism in the industry. However, if you are prepared to work hard, have endless enthusiasm and unbridled passion, then getting your break need not seem so impossible. But it's important to be realistic. Most sports journalists don't start out as sports journalists, the majority work in general assignment roles before navigating across to their chosen specialism. Also don't expect sports journalism to be a glamorous whirl of foreign assignments, prized seats at sold-out matches and getting to hang out with Posh and Becks. You are more likely to start covering Mangotsfield United than Manchester United or Arlesey rather than Arsenal. And if you see yourself as the next Henry Winter or Oliver Holt, remember there is an old journalism rule that 'you have to earn the right to have an opinion'.

You will also need to make the commitment to start reporting sport rather than watching it – which could mean giving up those Saturday afternoons with friends supporting your local football team. Be prepared for the antisocial hours as well. Sport happens in the evenings and at weekends, most sports journalists find their days off are frequently in the week, at the exactly the time all their friends and family are working. But don't expect or demand any sympathy and expect only envious looks when you talk about your job at parties. People view it in the same bracket as professional beer tasters – only travel writers get worse grief – and most people generally struggle to believe you actually get paid do it, rather than vice versa.

Nelly Bly and the five golden rules

Attitude is everything in journalism, if you don't have the right one then it doesn't matter how well you write. No one could ever accuse Nelly Bly of having a bad attitude. She was born in 1864 and always dreamed of being a reporter, but women hardly ever worked in newsrooms in the late 19th century and the very few that did were expected to only contribute to the arts and social pages. But Nelly was different and after earning a job at a rough and tough tabloid in New York, she set about making her mark. She'd heard reports of patient abuse at a local women's asylum but couldn't find the proof she needed to write the story. So she checked into a working-class boarding house and refused to go to bed – telling the boarders they were looking at her in a funny way and that they all seemed crazy. But they thought she was the crazy one and duly called the police. One court appearance later and Nelly was finally inside the asylum – as a patient. For more than a week, she suffered and chronicled the foul food, fouler conditions and patient abuse. When she got out her story, 'Ten Days in the Madhouse', caused a national sensation. The asylum was closed, the owners were arrested and the US government found nearly $1 million to contribute to women's mental health issues. Later in her career, Nelly suggested to her editor that she should mimic Jules Verne's book *Around the World in Eighty Days*. True to form, she completed the journey in 72 days and she was the only woman to file stories from the Eastern Front during the First World War.

Nelly represents five golden rules for getting on in journalism:

- She showed persistence. She didn't give up when the story got hard, she never took no for an answer.
- Nelly knew the importance of good sources. Sources are the most valuable and prized possession of any reporter. You never know if the non-league footballer you meet will become a Premier League star or the talented athlete, an Olympic champion. In the event of a house fire, a reporter should always save their contacts book first – then think about looking for the boyfriend, girlfriend, cat or dog.
- Nelly understood the importance of empathy. You need to be relatively hard-nosed in this job because contrary to popular opinion not all journalists think ethics is in the south of England. You can't interview a

mother who has lost a child, decorated war veteran who has had his medals stolen or an athlete whose hopes and dreams of success have just evaporated in a 10-second race unless you show a bit of feeling towards their circumstances.

- Nelly, like all good journalists should be, was inquisitive. Every day – as you travel to work or college, on the Tube or bus, you are surrounded by great stories. But some never get told because the people involved just don't get asked. Everyone has a story to tell and it's the true journalist that works out how to uncover it. People skills are vital to any reporter. As a default position people won't trust you, so you need to win their confidence and the best way to do that is if they like you.

- Good journalists need to be able to write. They need to be objective in their writing and present facts in the clearest and most concise way. Lots of people get into journalism because they enjoy writing. They are sometimes surprised about little of a reporter's day is spent at the keyboard – more of it will be dedicated to phoning contacts, interviewing, and researching. Newswriting is a harder skill than you think – and it doesn't come without training and a lot of practice. What most graduates – especially those on humanities degrees – find very hard is the art of using a single word instead of 10.

So after all that – do you still want to be a journalist? The hours can be long, the pay at starting level is hardly generous and the reality of the job is not so glamorous, but perseverance can be rewarded. But this is a competitive industry. There are more applicants than jobs – in such a climate, it is rare for editors to offer roles to candidates without basic training. Editors need to know you can turn around a tightly written 200-word story in rapid time. We need to know you've got a working knowledge of the law – and you aren't going to get us sued. In addition, most newspapers still look for reporters to have the industry standard of 100 words per minute for shorthand. You might think it's arcane in these days of MPG files and voice-translating software but shorthand remains the most efficient way of taking quick and accurate notes. Once learned, you'll never regret having the skill. It's also the best party trick.

So hard though it might be for you to swallow – after three years of university and a mountain of debt – but you will probably need more training but make sure any course you take will teach you the skills editors want. The National Council for the Training of Journalists (NCTJ) remains the industry standard – just look at the job adverts in the *Guardian*'s media section or on the website Hold the Front Page for evidence of this.

The NCTJ has been around since the early 1950s and its syllabus is set by editors rather than academics – making its a practical, vocational and relevant qualification. Its syllabus covers news writing, shorthand, media law and public affairs and gives the option to specialise in sports journalism, production journalism or video journalism, in addition to building a portfolio of published work. There are a variety of NCTJ-accredited courses around the UK – some are run by media organisations, such as News Associates or the Press Association, and taught in a fast-track format, taking an academic year and squeezing it into 20 intensive weeks, a more practical approach that can make the transition to the job more seamless. The press agency Sportsbeat also runs a 40-week sports-journalism training scheme, which includes all NCTJ examinations and placements on their news desk. But such intensive learning isn't right for everyone, so an academic year course might be more appropriate. An increasing number of universities offer an NCTJ qualification as part of a master's degree in journalism, while some – such as St Mary's University College and the University of Sunderland – even offer a sports journalism master's, which also includes all the NCTJ examination modules.

There are also numerous undergraduate courses in journalism, with an option to specialise in sports, and an increasing number of commercial providers, all teaching the NCTJ syllabus. In addition, there are other journalism courses, both at undergraduate and master's level, that are not part of the NCTJ framework. For example, Cardiff and City Universities are both home to highly respected schools of journalism with an impressive list of alumni.

The most important thing is to look far and wide at the range of courses available, make sure they are teaching the skills that editors want and, if in doubt, seek advice from those in the industry or online groups such as Wannabe Hacks, who aim to help aspiring journalists take their first steps into an industry that can appear quite daunting when you are on the outside looking in.

Some journalism courses don't teach shorthand to the industry standard of 100 words per minute and some don't teach shorthand at all – it's a skill that divides opinion. Of course, some sports reporters are able to work without it, but it's still highly prized by most editors. When jobs are so competitive, can you afford not to be as qualified as possible? 'Shorthand is critical for us,' said Andy Cairns, the editor of Sky Sports News. 'You don't have time to go over longhand notes when you are trying to be quicker than your rivals at getting a story out.' Sportsbeat's David Parsons adds:

I've got 20 staff reporters and every single one of them has shorthand. Given the importance of getting speedy quotes running as soon as possible, a candidate would have to be pretty sensational for me to consider them without this key skill. If I've got a stack of applications, it's very easy to eliminate those without shorthand. I believe that if you can apply yourself to learning shorthand then you are more likely to apply yourself to getting out a story.

Legal knowledge

As a journalist, there will be occasions when your legal knowledge is as important as your ability to craft an intro. You don't need to be a solicitor, but you do need to know how to keep your publication out of trouble – and your editor out of the courts or even prison. Press freedom is enshrined in our law, so it is vital to know how doggedly you can pursue a story without fear or favour and understand the full implications of what you are writing. You'll need to learn about journalists' defences against defamation and contempt and the restrictions that exist for reporting. Sports journalists frequently cover court cases and you should have a grasp of when the press can attend court, how reporting restrictions can be appealed and the limitations in place when covering cases involving sexual offences or children. Legal issues present themselves to journalists everyday – what is the difference between robbery and theft and libel and slander, for example?

You will also need to understand issues relating to copyright, breach of confidence, privacy and disclosure of sources, as well as broadcast regulations, which are becoming more and more relevant in the age of the multimedia journalist. A good qualification should not only equip you with the skills you need but show employers that you are serious and committed to journalism.

Before you spend valuable time and even more valuable money on training be absolutely sure this is the right job for you. Work experience is a good way of shedding any romanticised notion about the job and seeing what life as a reporter is really like. A newsroom can be a tough place – sometimes it can like Gordon Ramsay's kitchen but with worse language. But very few offices have the atmosphere of a newsroom as it lurches towards its deadline. It's an exciting place to be, especially if a big story is breaking all around you.

Work placements

If you do get a work placement – contribute and strike the right balance between keen and pushy. Don't just sit back and expect to be served up with work to do – be proactive and try to source your own stories. Even if they don't hit the mark, your efforts will still be appreciated and make you stand out. Research the media outlet you are working at in advance. It is incredible the number of times people on work experience sit down and ask, 'What exactly do you do here?' when they could have done some simple internet research in advance. Also make sure you find out about the dress code – some editors can be incredibly fastidious about this and first impressions are all important. Sportsbeat's David Jordan recalls:

> I never forget someone coming in for work experience in trainers and a Tottenham Hotspur shirt, the morning after Spurs had just won a north London derby. First, he obviously had a loose interpretation of smart casual and second he clearly didn't know our editor is an Arsenal fan.

Some people are put off journalism because even work experience placements can be hard to get – although those who give up at this first hurdle probably aren't suited to the industry anyway. Newspapers, magazines and agencies are inundated with requests for work experience – sports departments are also the most popular – so approach any contact in the same way you would an actual job application. Find out which person at the company is responsible for organising placements – and write them a personalised email. Journalists don't tend to have too many airs and graces but it's better to be conservative in the first instance, 'Dear Mr Toney' is better than 'Dear James', and 'Dear Sir or Madam' just underlines that you couldn't be bothered to do your research. Tailor your email to the outlet you are applying to and keep it short and snappy like a good story and whatever you do don't make any typos or sloppy grammatical errors. Journalists are busy, don't give them a reason not to look at you – attach your letter to the email but also paste it into the body text, where it will be easier to read. Try to demonstrate you've already shown a commitment to the industry too, by starting a blog and thinking about the content. Don't just write about a high-profile sports event that you've watched on the television – that requires minimal effort. Instead try your hand at a more offbeat feature, perhaps with your local football, cricket or rugby team. Get out and interview people and have a crack at writing quotes stories on your blog – no one will expect your work to be of a standard capable of being published by a professional news operation but potential employers will respect your attitude and be impressed by your decision to have a go.

Another good way of impressing is to volunteer at a local club as their press or media officer. It could be a local tennis club, darts league or cricket team. Often these organisations will submit reports to local press and providing them is a great way to come to the attention of journalists – and looks impressive when seeking work experience. You could also show off your digital skills to build them a website and generate multimedia content, such as video content for a YouTube channel. Time invested in this fledgling stage of your career could reap dividends in the future. The internet makes it easier to start building a portfolio.

Always remember when starting out that nothing is beneath you – turn your nose up and you will soon put others' noses out of joint. On placements you tend to spend your time shadowing or working on stories that are not priorities to staff journalists. Andrew Moorhouse, the head of journalism training at News Associates, said:

> There's a good story about one of our former trainees and his work placement. His editor gave him a story on a local community centre that was closing down and asked for just 100 words, for use as a NIB – or news in brief. On the face of it, it was quite a dull tale – a press release from the local council with a few lifeless quotes. But the aspiring reporter got on the phone. He tracked down a disabled theatre group, ballet classes, bridge clubs and various other organisations that used the facility and would now be homeless, until the replacement centre was built six months later.
>
> His editor – who was expecting a few paragraphs – got a dossier. He ran the story on the front page and the council gave the centre a stay of execution, so the theatre group could complete the production for which they'd been rehearsing so hard. That's not bad for days' work and it was no surprise the trainee made an impression and when a job was available, after he'd completed his NCTJ training, it was offered to him.

It might be wise to prepare an answer if asked why you want to be a sports journalist – and don't say, 'It would be nice to get paid for something I spend all my time watching.' Instead talk about the journalists that have inspired you and the stories that interest you. Good sports journalists are also good journalists, so seek a broad range of experience. Don't be one-dimensional and focus on sports journalism and nothing else. Try to build a portfolio of work that shows you are comfortable working across a variety of subjects; you will stand out better that way.

Remember that local weekly papers are traditionally places to go for work experience. Their staffs are smaller, so you are more likely to be given a chance to do some real reporting. But try to seek a placement somewhere where you will be given feedback on what you produce. Also, even if print journalism is your focus, look to broadcasting, in particular local radio, where you can broaden your skills. In addition, beware that a work placement at a larger organisation can be a great experience but you tend to spend more time shadowing than actually doing the job.

Now is the time to start thinking like a sports journalists and not a sports fan. Are you really prepared for something that you enjoy doing becoming your job? After all, passions tend to dull when something that once dominated every non-working moment just dominates every working moment. Will your love of football still shine so bright when you're covering your 80th match of the season, especially when it's likely a large percentage of those games will have been turgid encounters?

Meeting heroes is also a dangerous business. It's an old truth of sports journalism that they frequently disappoint and lose their lustre when they go from someone you admired to someone you just interviewed, especially if you 'asked for a word' and got exactly that and that word was 'no'.

Balance and objectivity are core components of journalism, so are you ready to be objective and set your allegiances aside? Just imagine you are writing an 'on the whistle' report about the team you've always supported. With two minutes to go, they are 2–0 down; do you really want the stress of a late comeback, the frantic rewrite and frayed nerves? The fan will say 'yes', but the journalist will almost certainly say 'no'. That's when you know you've made the transition from fan to reporter.

If you do take the plunge and decide that this is the career for you, then you have to do it with total conviction – someone whose effort is half-hearted will soon be found out, attitude and commitment can't be taught or learned. David Emery, the former *Daily Express* sports editor who now publishes four national sports titles, said:

> Sometimes experienced reporters can become a little complacent and that opens the way for young, enthusiastic journalist to make their name. The next phone call or question may be the one that provides the story, so never give up until you have exhausted all the possibilities. Energy and doggedness are two very important attributes for a journalist. Obviously you should be able to spell, have a proper understanding of syntax and a deep, rather than superficial, knowledge of sport is also important. Much of this can be learned though. What can't be taught so easily is a relentless wish to push yourself to be the best, no clock-watching, no leaving early for a date. This is a cut-throat profession at the top and only the most dedicated will make it.

But if that's not put you off and only doubled your determination, then it's worth checking out the Sports Journalists' Association website on a regular basis – and the annual subscription is well worth the money once you get that first job. The site posts job offers as they become available, while journalism news websites Hold the Front Page and Press Gazette, the latter also has a quarterly print edition and regular e-editions, are also good sources of information. The *Guardian*'s media section is probably the best place to catch up on industry gossip and is also recommended reading.

It's true that the hardest job to get in journalism is your first one. Once on the inside, it's easier to hear about positions that become available and make connections. Many positions are still not widely advertised, so don't miss the chance to make an impression when you go on work experience – journalists don't divulge their contacts easily but if they like you then they will be more likely to give you some tips and benefit of inside information. Sportsbeat's David Jordan says:

> I've not employed a junior reporter in the last four years that I've not already got to know. You need a qualification – I expect shorthand at 100 words per minute – but you need a brimming portfolio as well. Work experience is a great way to make your presence felt. It's a competitive industry, so we can afford to be very choosy. So stand out, make an effort and come across as a good team player.

Sorting out your CV

If you have an amusing or strange email address, now is the time to change it – it was very easy to discard an otherwise perfectly good curriculum vitae (CV) because the email address was 'armchairfootballhooligan@hotmail.com'. Keep it simple – no nicknames, just your name or variation of your name and number if required. Anything else is not professional.

As mentioned earlier, a blog is a prerequisite. Make sure its address is prominent at the top of your résumé beneath your address and contact details and make sure it's up to date when you send out your CV.

Now is also the time to delete anything you might find embarrassing on your Twitter account or Facebook – they will get looked at. If you wouldn't email the content directly to your prospective employer, then don't put it online. Perhaps consider having one Twitter account for your friends and family and another for work purposes, which you follow people of interest, retweet interesting stories that shows a breadth of reading and comment on news issues but check your spelling. It may also be the time to double-check your privacy settings on Facebook.

Compress less relevant and older jobs, and any periods of temping – unless it is relevant to the job you are applying for. Remember jobs attract large numbers of applicants and an application for a junior-reporting position should not run longer than two pages of A4. Some recruitment consultants recommend applying a two-second test, in which you can learn about the candidate from just a quick scan. When writing an intro, your challenge is to get the reader to read on and the same applies to a CV. Just as you would when writing a story, avoid lengthy paragraphs. The use of bullet points is fine. Keep sentences concise and punchy and avoid jargon and abbreviations. Put your journalism skills at the top of the first page. If you've gained an NCTJ certificate or equivalent journalism degree, put that before anything else. In addition, make sure the editor knows immediately whether you've got shorthand and at what speed – be prepared for this to be checked during interviews. Obviously, list your university, if you attended, and the degree you achieved. It's worth listing A-level results but GCSEs are less relevant and can be condensed; for example: 10 GSCEs – including English Language and Literature (A) – grades A–C.

Be truthful

You should never lie on a CV – many an interview has fallen flat because a candidate has gilded their résumé by listing conversational French as a language skill, only for the interviewer to open up with, 'Depuis combien de temps avez-vous voulu être un journaliste?' However, do not volunteer negative information – there is no requirement to list courses that you started but did not finish or exams you failed. Some titles, especially those in areas not well served by transport links, will also insist on a driving licence – so make sure this information is prominent.

Opinion is divided about mission statements – some editors believe it's useful to see candidates summarise themselves in short and succinct language; others think they add little.

Too often the majority claim the prospective employee is a hard-working, enthusiastic and committed team player – which you would hope is a given. Be a little more focused with something like, 'NCTJ-qualified journalism graduate with work experience across a range of local and regional press, television and radio, seeking a role as a sports reporter'. Obviously, this can be adapted depending on the type of media organization you are approaching. It might also be an idea to sum up your skills in one place, using headings and bullet points for added emphasis:

Journalism	Software
* Reporting	* Experience of content management systems
* Shorthand (100 wpm)	* QuarkXPress and Adode InDesign
* Media Law	* Adobe Final Cut Pro and Pinnacle
* Production	* Abode Photoshop

If listing software, focus on software used by journalists for page production and video and photo editing. Most employers would take it for granted that a candidate will be proficient in standard programme like Microsoft Word or Excel.

However, the only real rule is to keep your CV simple. Editors don't care if you used to work in a DIY store on Saturdays or behind the bar of your local pub on a Friday night. They are more interested in work experience and placements, so list these as high as possible. Summarise your roles, responsibilities and achievements in succinct bullet points. Strike a balance between being boastful and too modest and avoiding 'I' and 'me', which forces you to make each point start with a power word. For example:

- Edited student monthly student newspaper and four annual supplements.
- Managed team of 20 student journalists and appointed a management team including a deputy editor, chief subeditor, features editor and sports editor.
- Nominated for student journalism awards in four categories and was highly commended in the scoop of the year category.

Most importantly is double and triple-check your information, because you cannot afford a single sloppy typographical error. It's also surprising the amount of time people get their own telephone numbers wrong.

Some candidates take a wacky approach – one editor recalls being sent a teabag with an application, with the implication that the aspiring reporter would be happy to make the tea. About one in ten editors might find this attention-grabbing, but it would turn the other nine cold, so be conservative.

There is no need for a photo on a CV. It's best to use black ink on white paper and select a common straightforward font. Don't try to cram too much on two pages by using a small font – Arial at point-size 11 is sufficient – and use bold or italics sparingly and consistently. You might make headings bold, such as 'Education', and italicise publications, such as the *Daily Telegraph*.

Most CVs are submitted by email so choose a common format for your attachment, such as a Word document. Even better, supply it as a PDF file. Remember you don't need to list your date of birth, although if you are applying for a junior position there is no harm in doing so. In addition, listing hobbies is largely irrelevant, unless you think these add to your desirability as a candidate, for example charity or volunteering work.

Many editors would rather see the names of your referees rather than 'References on request' written on your CV – in an industry such as journalism there is a chance your potential employer knows, or knows of, the referees you have selected. References from a family member or a landlord of a pub where once you once pulled pints is no good – ideally make both your referees relevant to journalism, perhaps a course tutor and an editor or journalist from work experience.

Going freelance

Some journalists look to freelance – work for a variety of outlets rather than committing themselves to a staff job. It can be a tough existence – there is no guarantee where the next pay cheque is coming from and working from home and not having an employer to support you can be lonely and challenging. There is no editor or colleague to turn to for advice, no post-work drinks or office Christmas party. Some, who have been journalists for a number of years on staff positions, elect to move into freelancing because the flexibility suits their lifestyle. They have an advantage because they will have already built up a network of contacts and will be known to editors who might commission them. Others will combine freelance reporting with casual shift work, usually working as subeditors on production teams. However, it's worth noting that freelance budgets are always cut before staff budgets and recent years have seen rates for reporting and production shifts at most major news outlets remain static or even go down.

If you want to work freelance, check out websites such as sportsjournalists. co.uk, which is run by the Sports Journalists' Association, and research industry rates for jobs, which fluctuate widely depending on titles. It's much harder to break into freelancing as a junior or recently qualified reporter, although not impossible. You will have to be as good a salesperson as you are a reporter, you will need to enjoy networking and keep on top of invoicing and, as you are likely to be paid on a self-employed basis, you will be responsible for your own tax affairs. Indeed, most freelancers say that managing their own financial affairs remains the most frustrating aspect of the job – they don't want to hassle those who commission them for fear they won't be commissioned in the future.

Make sure you agree a payment for a job in advance and check what the publication's payment terms are – they should not be any longer than 30 days. Also agree terms – if they ask you for 800 words but, for reasons of space, only use 400 what will they pay? The temptation, especially when you are starting out as a freelancer, is that you are so desperate to secure a commission that the issue of money can be swept aside. But life as a freelancer will be short unless you can make it pay – so invoice promptly, remind politely and don't be afraid to take action.

However, there will be periods when you are working long days – because you will not want to turn down work – while at other times you may have too much free time. Will Unwin, who graduated from an NCTJ training course just under two years ago and now works freelance for a number of outlets, including newspapers, agencies, magazines and websites, has the following advice about working freelance:

> The difference between a freelance journalist and one in a staff position is that you have to be as flexible as possible in order to get shift work or matches to cover. You need a good body of work to prove your trustworthiness as a writer, as people assume you will be able write in the publication's style straight away. You get your reward in being slightly better paid than staffers, but without guarantee of work.
>
> If necessary apply for work experience, prove your ability to the employer and then badger them for shifts etc. Once you've got a door ajar, you can easily make more contacts, covering a Premier League game puts you in contact with dozens of journalists in similar positions who are more than happy to point youngsters in the right direction. But without contacts you're nothing, various parts of the industry are still 'it's not what you know …' sectors. Ask your friends in the right places to help you out, which is a useful avenue if you know the right people.

As a freelancer, it is certainly worth thinking about joining an official organisation such as the Sports Journalists' Association, which also gives you the option to apply for an International Sports Press Card, recognised internationally and administered by the Association Internationale De La Presse Sportive (AIPS).

You might also consider membership of either the National Union of Journalists (NUJ) or British Association of Journalists (BAJ) which offer legal advice to members, sometimes vital for freelancers, and give you the ability to apply for the National Press Card, which is recognised by most official organisations, including the police.

APPENDIX

JOURNALISM ETHICS

Journalism ethics and press standards are under the microscope now more than ever before. Most media organisations insert a code of conduct into their terms and conditions of employment and freelancers should also be wary of the legal and ethical parameters of their work, whether they work in newspapers, magazines or online.

All members of the press have a duty to maintain the highest professional standards with regards to accuracy, harassment, reporting of crimes, undercover journalism and, of course, privacy. A journalist must take care not to publish inaccurate, misleading or distorted information, including pictures. Mistakes should be correctly promptly and, where appropriate, an apology be published.

Press freedoms recognise that journalists are allowed to be partisan but it is important that there is always a clear distinction between comment, conjecture and fact.

Everyone is entitled to respect for his or her private and family life, home, health and correspondence, including digital communications, while it is also important to seek consent from a parent or similarly responsible adult when interviewing or photographing children under the age of 16. The most topical issue for press standards covers the use of clandestine devices and subterfuge, in the light of the phone-hacking scandal that caused the closure of Britain's biggest selling newspaper, *News of the World*. The press must not seek to obtain or publish material acquired by using hidden cameras or clandestine listening devices or by intercepting private or mobile telephone calls, messages or emails.

Journalists should not use information about which they are privy for their own financial profit in advance of its publication and they also have a moral obligation to protect the confidentiality of their sources. Reporting should also never demonstrate prejudice or reinforce stereotypes with regards to race, gender, age, sexuality or disability.

Of course, there are always exceptions to the above, particularly when the newspaper is able to claim a defence of public interest. For example, they may claim that secret recordings are the only way to detect or expose a crime or serious impropriety or they are preventing the public from being misled by an action or statement of an individual or organisation.

It is important to be aware of the code and to be able to satisfy yourself that your reporting methods are honest, legal and transparent and your copy is fair, balanced and objective.

JOURNALISM AND COPYRIGHT

It is important that journalists understand issues relating to copyright and they are usually covered in detail on the media law syllabus of journalism training courses. If you work for a publication, it is likely that you will have assigned your rights to copyright to your employer, which will allow them the ability to commercialise the content, for example via syndication. As a freelancer, you will own your copyright so be wary of any attempt to make you sign it away.

All material, written, broadcast and photography, is protected by copyright legislation, which for work originating in the European Union, lasts 70 years after the death of its author. Copyright can be bought, sold, transferred or licensed but, in certain circumstances, no permission is needed. It is possible to use copyrighted material for research, criticism, review or reporting current events and the publication of excerpts, usually quotes, is permitted provided they are attributed and their original source acknowledged. The internet makes abuse of copyright harder to police, but the same laws apply to online news services as they do to traditional media. Copyright law can be complicated, so if in doubt, seek advice.

PROFESSIONAL ORGANISATIONS

There are a number of organisations dedicated to providing professional services for journalists and sports journalists.

Membership of the Sports Journalists' Association is restricted to professional reporters reporters, editors and photographers. Its website – www.sportsjournalists.co.uk – is a good source of information about the industry, particularly job moves and vacancies. It represents the interests of its members in discussions with sporting bodies, for example, arguing for improvements in press facilities or issues regarding media accreditation. Membership entitles a sports journalist to apply for an International Sports Press Card, distributed by the Association Internationale De La Presse Sportive (AIPS) – www.aipsmedia.com. This is widely recognised by event organisers, but it comes with no guarantee of accreditation.

Journalists may seek to join a union, such as the National Union of Journalists (NUJ), British Association of Journalists (BAJ) or Chartered Institute of Journalists (CIOJ), while some organisations have staff associations, which represent the interests of employees with management.

GLOSSARY

Journalism, like many industries, has a language all of its own. It is not too complicated though and pretty easy to pick up. So when someone on the backbench tells you, 'We're off stone early tonight so we need to have your copy filed by 8 and will add quotes later,' you will soon understand what is meant.

Above the fold – The top half of a page on a newspaper or the first few stories displayed on a website. It is where the best stories are positioned.

Add – An addition to a story already written or in the process of being written.

Accreditation – A media pass or credential required to cover an event and give access to media facilities and athletes.

Agent – A sports agent is a person who procures and negotiates employment and endorsement contracts for a player.

Angle – The angle is the point or theme of a news or feature story.

Archive – All media extensively archive all the material they, or their rivals, publish for research purposes. Much of this is now online but some publications maintain a library, often referred to as the 'morgue'.

Backbench – The senior management of a publication or media outlet, which normally includes the editor, deputy editor, news editor and chief subeditor.

Beat – The area or specialism assigned to a reporter.

Breaking story – A news story that is currently developing.

Briefing – A meeting, phone call, email etc. in which journalists are told information for background purposes – usually by press officers or media managers.

Byline – A line that includes the name of the reporter or reporters who wrote the story.

Catchline – A name given to a story to distinguish it from others, for example USOPENFEDERER

Correspondent –Usually a senior reporter, not office based.

Closed question – A badly phrased question that could elicit a single-word answer, for example, 'You must be very disappointed to lose that match?'

Colour piece – A descriptive piece, normally taking a different angle from event coverage, that can have opinion threaded through it. Normally written by senior reporters, such as the chief sportswriter.

Conference – A regular meeting conducted by the editor, usually involving his or her backbench and senior staff, in which stories and upcoming events are discussed and planned.

Contact – A trusted person who provides information to a journalist, sometimes off the record. Journalists keep their contacts' mobile numbers and email addresses in their contacts book.

Copy – The main text of a journalist's story.

Copy advisory – A note sent to an editor or issued to a client, informing them about issues with a story. For example, 'It's just been raining at the cricket and they're shortening the game to 32 overs. Estimated finish time is now 7 p.m.'

Copytaker – A telephonist who takes in copy over the phone when a reporter can't file by email.

CMS – Content Management System; the password-protected back office of a website, where stories, pictures and video are uploaded and content is ordered and scheduled. There are many types of CMS, Drupal being one of the most popular.

Dateline – If a reporter is filing from abroad they will add a dateline to the story – for example, 'From Sarah Smith, in New York'.

Deadline – The law by which journalists live. The latest time that copy should be received or a newspaper might go to press.

Diary – The bible by which a sports desk is run. Also the name of offbeat columns covering sports news or behind-the-scenes activity at major events.

Draft – The first version of an article before it's submitted to an editor and edited.

Embargo – A fixed time after which journalists are allowed to publish information provided to them in advance. For example, the Queen's New Year honours list is made available for story-gathering purposes but stories cannot be published until midnight on 31 January.

Ezine – A specialised online magazine.

Exclusive – A story that is obtained and breaks in advance of rival media.

Fact file – A column of facts presented to add depth and context that runs in conjunction with a story.

Feature – A story that emphasises the human or entertaining aspects of a situation. It's longer and more detailed than a news story and has plenty of background information.

Filing – The act of sending your story to your editor.

Follow-up – A story that expands on an earlier story. If the Chelsea manager resigns and you write that story, a follow-up will be a story discussing the merits of potential successors.

Freelancer – A self-employed journalist who works for a number of media outlets.

Gaggle – An informal press conference, usually a gathering of reporters around a player or coach after an event.

Headline – The main title of the article. In newspapers, a headline must grab the reader and get his or her interest in the story. Online, a headline must be optimised for internet search engines.

Intro – The all-important first paragraph of a story; it must be snappy and succinct. Sometimes referred to as your lead. If your editor thinks you haven't angled your story correctly they may say, 'You've buried the lead.'

Internship – When a student, usually in college, works for a set period for a print, broadcast or outline news outlet. The purpose of the internship is to give the student experience working for a professional news organization. Internships can be paid and unpaid.

Kill – To prevent a story from running. A kill fee may also be paid to a freelancer for a story that has been commissioned but not published by a media outlet.

Laptop – All sports reporters will have a laptop to file their copy from remote events. Make sure if has a long battery life because power points can be in short supply at venues.

Long lead – 'Lead' describes the amount of time that a journalist has between receiving a writing assignment and submitting the completed piece. A long lead story will be compiled over several weeks or months.

Live blog – A type of blog in which someone reports live from an event by posting short entries during the event.

Mixed zone – In major events, a mixed zone for radio and television journalists is made available near the podium. In this area, athletes can be interviewed after the official ceremony. The positions of the media representatives are defined by the organiser in accordance with an order of priority.

MTF – More to follow; reporters should write 'MTF' on the bottom of stories if they have further information to file. If they have concluded their copy they should write '-ends-'.

NCTJ – National Council for the Training of Journalists; this long-running journalism training scheme is the most respected in the UK. It is taught in a number of accredited centres, including working news organisations, universities, further education providers and commercial centres.

NIB – News in brief; a quick summary of a story.

Off diary – A term applied to an unpredicted story that is not scheduled in the diary. An off-diary story could be the sudden dismissal of a coach or a reporter who has brought in an agenda-setting exclusive.

Off the record – Information given to a journalist as background on condition that it will not be used in a story or, alternatively, information given to a journalist for use in a story on condition that the source will not be identified.

On the record – Information given by a source or contact who has agreed to be identified in the story.

Off stone – An old term, dating back to printing techniques, for the final time a newspaper must be sent to the printers.

On spec – An article that is written 'just in case', but it will only be used if needed.

One-on-one – An exclusive interview not shared with other media.

Open question – A well-phrased question that avoids the interviewee giving a yes or no answer, for example, 'How would you assess your second-half performance?'

Opinion piece – Articles that don't have to be balanced, so they can be partisan, unlike news stories. Usually written in column form by a senior reporter.

Outro – The final line in a story that neatly rounds it off and might refer back to the intro.

On the whistle – Copy filed immediately after an event finishes, regardless of any late developments.

Page lead – The main story on a page of a newspaper or section of a website. It's positioning is decided by the editor or senior staff.

Press agency – A news service that provides a range of content to many different outlets.

Press conference – When reporters are gathered to question someone in the news, usually taking it in turns to ask questions. Such events are usually organised by an individual or company to deal with all the media in one session.

Press release – Information released to the media for publication, usually sent via email and sometimes subject to an embargo.

Press tribune – Also known as the press box, this is the area reserved for sports journalists to watch an event. General public are not allowed and it must be treated as a working area.

Public relations – Commonly known as PR; a discipline of the media that looks after reputation, with the aim of earning understanding and support, and influencing opinion and behaviour.

Portfolio – Where a journalist keeps a collection of his or her best published work. Often an editor will ask to see your portfolio, especially if recruiting for junior positions.

Profile – A piece that is an in-depth look at an individual or organisation.

Ratings – Sports journalists may be asked to provide ratings at an event. For example, it could involve scoring football players out of 10 in a football match and giving a brief description of each one's contribution.

Refresh – An updated story with additional information included that wasn't available when it was first published. It is common to get a story running online and then refresh it as it develops.

Reported speech – An interviewee's words paraphrased by the reporter with no quotation marks. For example: McCoy insisted he had no ill feelings towards his rival but vowed to reverse the result at Cheltenham later this year.

Round table – When a number of journalists interview together, usually when time would not permit an athlete to give a number of one-on-ones.

Running copy – A report filed in a number of takes as an event is ongoing, usually asked for when a deadline is very tight, allowing production staff to be working on copy rather than waiting for it to all arrive at once.

Schedule – Upcoming events to be covered by sport desks and a rota of reporters and production staff. Most sports operations operate a shift system, with many operating 24/7.

Shorthand – An abbreviated symbolic writing method that increases speed or brevity of writing as compared to a normal method of writing a language. The most popular form of shorthand for journalists is Teeline and the industry standard is 100 words per minute.

Source – An individual who provides information for a story.

Splash – The lead story of a publication, usually on the front or back page, or the top item on a website.

Sidebar – A story that runs alongside a lead giving extra information and depth. For example, the sidebar to a football match report might include quotes from managers and players.

Staffer – A journalist who is directly employed by a main organisation. They will always take preference over freelancers.

Stringer – A freelance journalist hired on an ad hoc basis to cover events.

Subeditor – The person who checks and edits a reporter's work for accuracy and legal issues, and is responsible for headlines.

Tip – Information passed to a reporter, normally off the record and in confidence.

Twitter – A service that allows users to send messages up to 140-characters long to 'friends' via mobile Short Message Service (SMS), website or Instant Messenger (IM).

Vox pops – From the Latin *vox populi*; short interview clips with people to add colour to a story. For example, you might use clips from five former players talking about a new coach of a team or five fans giving their thoughts on a recent match or performance.

Work placement – Time, normally a few days or a couple of weeks, spent at a media organisation, often while studying a formal journalism qualification, where you put theory into practice and build your portfolio.

Wires – Agencies that provide all their content to subscriber titles, such as the Press Association, Reuters and Agence France-Presse (AFP).

INDEX

Page numbers that include an f refer to figures.